ANDREW GUMMI
European football as ...
when he and his mates lost 36-0 to a village youth team
somewhere in Germany. He studied Russian at university
in the era of world-renowned players like Oleg Blokhin,
Rinat Dasaev, Margaret Thatcher and Ronald Reagan,
becoming familiar with the dental structure of Soviet and
East German guard dogs and supporting teams like
Bohemians Prague, Rapid Vienna and Dinamo Minsk on
their road to eternal obscurity. He spent months at a time
as a student in Germany, Austria and Brezhnev's Soviet
Union (twice - Minsk and Kiev) before joining a branch
of the Foreign Office as an East European specialist. He
is an occasional contributor to *When Saturday Comes*
and lives in Gloucestershire with his wife and young
daughter. If he had three wishes, he's sad enough for one
of them to be for an Icelandic team to win the UEFA
Champions' League, but admits he's probably in for a
long wait on that one.

You Come With Me - I get tickets

On the football terraces with the locals in 15 European countries

ANDREW GUMMER

The Parrs Wood Press
Manchester

First Published 2004

THE PARRS WOOD PRESS
St Wilfrid's Enterprise Centre
Royce Road, Manchester, M15 5BJ
www.parrswoodpress.com

ISBN: 1 903158 53 2

Printed and bound in Spain

*I didn't actually find many facts,
but I had a good time.*

Former Sports Minister Tony Banks, returning from
a pre-World Cup fact-finding mission in Japan, August 2000.

ACKNOWLEDGEMENTS

Many people helped me with this book: too many to mention all by name, and some of them without really knowing it, but special thanks go to: Tapani Olkkuu, Martin Smutov, Marcin Sobczak, Anthony Egwuatu, Hakan Johansson, Sorin Arotaritei, Romeo Ionescu, the staff at Olympic Airlines in Sofia, or some of them anyway; Karina Boikovska, Sven Wiese, Buffo Schnaedelbach, Vassilis Arapidis, Oleg Komlyakov, Ilya Solovev, Yulia Soloveva, Anatoly and Lilya, Geir Thorsteinsson, Zaal Guiguineishvili, Rati Chelidze, Dato Buachidze, Dima Nhavchanidze, Stuart Christie, Roland at Betsy's in Tbilisi, Muraz, Marko, Vlatka Jandel, Igor Kramarsic, Josip Mihovil, Andrey Troyan, Doctor Zoom, The Football Association of Turkey, Erdinc Sivretepe, Steve Wilson, Mary Betley, Graham Doe, for pointing out the kangaroo; Jan Stafford, Jane McNeir, Colin White, Andy Ellis, Andy at PWP, Marcus Robson, my wife Melanie and both our families; and finally Maia, without whom this book (a) could have been completed at least a year earlier, but more importantly (b) may never have been written at all.

CONTENTS

1 Anyone Remember Dukla Prague? 9

2 What Price You Want To Pay? .13
Finland - Albania, Helsinki, 2 September 2000

3 That's Ott. Everyone Respects Him 24
Estonia - Portugal, Tallinn, 3 September 2000

4 Widzew Hool's 35
Poland - Belarus, Lodz, 7 October 2000

5 Oh No. Now We Dance 48
Norway - Ukraine, Oslo, 11 October 2000

6 Aye, They'll Get A Few, Right Enough 58
Belgium - San Marino, Brussels, 28 February 2001

7 I Finish Early, Today Is Football 66
Romania - Italy, Bucharest, 24 March 2001

8 No, You Must Pay Cash 85
Greece - Germany, Athens, 28 March 2001

9 You Have No Ticket? Pfffhh! .98
Netherlands - Cyprus, Eindhoven, 25 April 2001

10 Endrew, Frankly Speaking, Are You Eriksson Fen? .107
Russia - Yugoslavia, Moscow, 2 June 2001

11 Looks Like He's Putting Up One Of The Nets 121
Iceland - Bulgaria, Reykjavik, 6 June 2001

12 In Tbilisi We Have Not Footboll!! 131
Georgia - Hungary, Tbilisi, 1 September 2001

13 Why You See This Game? 146
Hungary - Romania, Budapest, 5 September 2001

14 Dinamo Are Political Club .150
Croatia - Belgium, Zagreb, 6 October 2001

15 I am Doctor Zoom 163
Ukraine - Germany, Kiev, 10 November 2001

16 Number 10 Is Hagi Number 178
Turkey - Austria, Istanbul, 14 November 2001

1.

Anyone Remember Dukla Prague?

IT'S ALL THE FAULT of the people who write travel guidebooks. If it hadn't been for the way they included all the wrong information, I wouldn't have gone to all these places.

I never wanted to know what was in the art galleries. I wasn't half as interested as the books were in monuments to long-dead poets. I didn't want to go on sightseeing tours or buy souvenirs. I wanted to know what the real people who lived in these places actually did. I wanted to know all the things few guidebooks ever think you want to know.

Too often, the compilers' assumption appeared to be that if you were interested in travelling to a big city, as opposed to a beach resort, you must be a culture vulture, and that meant museums, galleries and opera houses, not music venues, beer or football stadiums. It meant what used to be important in the city's life, not what was important in the inhabitants' lives today. It meant history, rather than anything contemporary. It meant the city, not the people; the inanimate rather than the animate.

I wanted to cut through the remote, highbrow stuff, and find out about the people whose city I was in. It felt a bit like the 'No Nonsense' ads on TV for John Smith's bitter, only arguably with added brain cells. I wanted to do what the locals did, and to blend in so that they would stop me in the street and ask for directions, not the other way round. Forget the opera tickets priced out of the reach of the locals, and to hell with the national costumes and the priceless pottery in the museums - I wanted to get out and see what today's locals did with their lives. Which were their favourite bars? How did they get home and out to work again the next day? Did they read newspapers on the train like we did? Did they like the same kind of music as me? If not, what sort of music did they like? Where did they go to hear it, and what was so good about it? What kind of cars were on the roads? Were they locally-built or just second-hand German ones? Did they stop at zebra crossings? What did local people wear? Were they outgoing or reserved? Did they live life outdoors whenever they could? And why do so many Russian men under 30 have skinhead haircuts and 'Black Sabbath' tattoos?

Look in any travel guide for, say, France. I bet you'll find more text about minor art galleries in a provincial city than about football in the country as a whole - and yet from 2000 to 2002 the French national side were simultaneously European and World Champions. Sport, and spectator sport in particular, appears to be almost taboo. The most that any guidebook will ever tell you is that football is the main spectator sport (unless it's cycling or basketball or something) and that 'international games take place regularly'. Well OK, but how regularly? And what about domestic games? How do you get tickets for any of them? What's it like when you get there? The guidebooks beg so many questions.

As a student, the first few football games I watched in person outside England made each place appear that much more vivid, real and lived in. I was getting insights into what made each country different just by seeing how the locals watched, and I found that if you talked to them, they talked back. Fans in the old Soviet Union took the chance to have a good shout and vent some of life's frustrations in a way that no other aspect of everyday life in the USSR seemed to allow. I was once in Austria to see Rapid Vienna against Dinamo Kiev in the UEFA Cup, and then a year or two later I saw Arsenal get thrashed 5-2 at home by Spartak Moscow, in Terry Neill's last game in charge. This was the early 1980s and both games represented the Cold War on the football field - plucky West European sides up against monoliths of Soviet orthodoxy. Believe me, the Kiev side of that era didn't win prizes for tactical innovation.

ANYONE REMEMBER DUKLA PRAGUE?

It's said that radio fires the imagination more vividly than television precisely because of the lack of pictures - you must create and supply your own, based on what you hear. Every radio commentary I heard as a kid involving teams from abroad (on what the BBC, in those days, rather quaintly called 'European Soccer Special') appeared to pit Liverpool against teams like Dukla Prague, the Czech Army side - our British boys holding back the hostile, gimlet-eyed hordes of communism on a stormy night in Prague. Or else it was Dai Davies in the Wrexham goal, keeping the Welsh team in it single-handed. Those were the days when teams like Dinamo Tbilisi and Steaua Bucharest could still win big UEFA competitions, the days before the money men came along in the 1990s to iron out football's tiresome unpredictabilities, buying all the talent and tilting the playing field forever in favour of the same dozen or so elite West European clubs.

Club football, and its money, dominate the UEFA scene now. Toys leave club managers' prams at high speed, especially around Highbury and Manchester, whenever the national team tail tries to wag the domestic club dog. Yet much of Europe's football public outside England, Spain, Germany or Italy finds the international scene more compelling than their own club football, because their country's team has a chance. Cyprus can beat Spain, France can crash out of the World Cup finals at the group stage despite winning their last two major tournaments; a bobble-hatted Faroese goalkeeper is on the winning side against Austria, while tiny Slovenia see off mighty Russia and Macedonia make England look very overpaid and ordinary in Southampton. Where are the upsets like that in club football?

When the qualifying groups for Korea/Japan 2002 were drawn, I saw an opportunity. I was in a position to be flexible with my day job, so I could get to some of European football's outposts, even in midweek, and see for myself what made the locals tick. I wanted to get to as many qualifying games as possible, and I also wanted them to be as far as possible off UEFA's well-beaten, brightly lit, commercial track. If I saw big name countries play, I wanted it to be when they were away from home and vulnerable, somewhere with a bumpy pitch, dodgy food, inadequate floodlights and a vibrant atmosphere created by locals eager to see the big boys fall flat on their faces. How sharp were the guard dogs' teeth in Bucharest? What, if anything, would make even an Icelander stand up and shout? How did you go about getting tickets for Turkey against Austria when your local team plays in Nationwide Division Three? What were Greek hot dogs like? And most importantly, what were the fans like, the people who actually went and stood on the terraces? What songs did they sing? Did they stick behind their country or turn against them when the going got tough? Did they carry domestic club rivalries into the international scene? Did they all think English football was the bees' knees? How much did they care about the game? Here was my chance to find out.

2.

What Price You Want To Pay?

Finland-Albania, Finnair Stadium, Helsinki, Saturday 2 September 2000

I WASN'T READY. We'd just had the worst imaginable holiday in Wales, with it raining every day, our two-year-old daughter going bonkers at being kept in, our friends' two kids doing the same a few miles up the road, and us all ending up hiring Disney videos to prevent them all from killing each other. Our friends' house seemed to have been built above an underground river. Even the mice wore wellies, and Marcus said it was the first time he'd seen gills on a woodlouse.

So I'd been too busy hanging everything (and everyone) out to dry to spend much time thinking about the first round of competitive World Cup qualifying match dates that September. But I had at least spotted that Finland, in England's qualifying group, were playing on the Saturday, and Estonia on the Sunday. As the two countries are just a short boat trip apart, there would be plenty of time to see both games.

Provided I had a ticket. The Finnish FA didn't reckon on selling English fans all that many tickets for the Albania game, so, not for the only time, I turned to the locals for help. I made contact with a few of Finland's committed fans (they do exist), and one of them pointed me towards an outfit called Lippupalvelu, which translates as Ticket Service, or similar. But they didn't answer my e-mails and their website was all in Finnish, which I grudgingly had to admit was fair enough, given that they exist to provide Finnish people with tickets for events taking place in Finland. I couldn't even tell if you could book by credit card. So I rang them up.

'I want to buy a ticket for the Finland-Albania World Cup clash in about 10 days' time,' I said.

There was a long pause.

'You want ticket for Finland-Albania?'

'Yes, that's right.'

'Where are you calling from?'

'England,' I said, wondering what business that was of hers.

'Why you want ticket for Finland-Albania? We play England only in October. September is Albania game.'

'I'm going to be in Helsinki that weekend anyway and thought I'd go to the match.'

There was a pause while she processed this information. I decided not to tell her the only reason I was going to be in Helsinki at all was to go to the match, and that moreover I'd already paid plenty of non-refundable money for a plane ticket all the way there and back. I thought if she knew this, she'd refuse to sell me a ticket on the pretext of excluding people of unsound mind from her country.

'It's not easy to find even one ticket,' she said, clearly still trying to decide whether I was (a) mad, (b) a timewaster, or (c) both of the above. If she'd actually asked, I could have told her the answer was (a).

'What price you want to pay?' she asked finally.

'Well, how much are the tickets?' I asked.

'We have 80 markka, 140, 200 and 300 markka.' Take off one zero and you've got the price in pounds, give or take.

'What kind of view do you get for 80 markka?'

'For 80, very bad. Very very bad. All of those tickets have been sold.'

Wondering what this said about Finnish spectators, I splashed out on a 200 markka ticket, which turned out to be in the Finnair Plus Silver Block 131, Rivi 2 Paikka 6. Was this Row 2 Seat 6, or Row 6 Seat 2? I'd find out.

WHAT PRICE YOU WANT TO PAY?

As we left Stansted, I noticed that half the passengers for my flight were wearing kilts.

'I'm hoping to get to every country in Europe to see Scotland play by the time I'm 35,' Andrew told me from the row behind mine. He and most of this planeload were on their way to Riga for Scotland's game with Latvia. 'It's a must-win game,' said his friend alongside him. I think that's what he said. His accent sounded like he was rolling his letter 'r's even in a sentence like that without a letter 'r' anywhere in it. 'We cannae afford to drop any points on this one.' He thought if Scotland got a result against Latvia that weekend and, crucially, away to Croatia in a month's time, they were as good as on the plane to Korea/Japan.

'How come you're going to Latvia this way?' I asked Andrew. Scotland to Latvia via Essex and Finland seemed kind of a roundabout route.

'I've no idea,' he said. 'It wasn't me that fixed the travel. So far I've been on four trains, had two taxi rides and been on three buses, and that's just to get to Stansted. When we get to Finland we'll have to get the catamaran across to Tallinn and then we can think about how we get across Estonia into Latvia. That border's dodgy, you know. Plus the mafia have started bombing in Riga.' This was true - a bomb had gone off in the city two or three weeks before and all the evidence pointed to gangland disputes. 'I think we're just going to find a minibus in Tallinn, give the driver $100 and tell him to take us.'

This bunch clearly had a fair few away trips under their belt. I'd not met football fans before with quite such an in-depth knowledge of obscure Balkan airlines that would fly you to Sarajevo on a Sunday, or who had an opinion on whether Bucharest or Skopje was worse when it came to hails of rocks being thrown at your coach by hostile locals, upset that you don't support their team.

'The police in Minsk were great,' said the lad beside Andrew. 'We really needed them after that game. They came up to us and said, "We're going to escort you back to your hotel, because it's nasty out there." We said, "Thanks all the same, but we're Scots, and we don't need escorting to the hotel. But can you escort us to the pub?"'

15

YOU COME WITH ME - I GET TICKETS

I pointed out that they could see the Estonia game in Tallinn the day after the Latvia one. But the whole plane knew this already, and so did the hundreds of Scots already basing themselves in Tallinn. Estonia and Scotland have a footballing history, after the floodlights fiasco in the match between them a few years ago. But no one on the plane had a bad word for Tallinn or the Estonians. 'Tallinn's just like Prague,' said Andrew, 'it's a super city.' He then told me where all the best Irish bars were and warned me about prostitutes in the big hotels. At least I think it was a warning.

I left them all at Helsinki airport, got a bus into town and fixed up a hotel. I'd got up at three that morning so I awarded myself the job of spending a demanding afternoon in various open air cafes and on a boat round some of the islands in the archipelago. I sat in the sun and read the various What's On magazines I'd picked up, which didn't have a huge amount in them apart from reviews of newly-opened Lappish and Uzbekistani restaurants. I also flicked through a publication for the city's more entrepreneurial Russian guests, the agenda-setting *Biznes Bez Granits*, or *Business Without Frontiers*, which had advertisements for how you could build your own Finnish-style wooden house for only $750, and interviews with alarmingly well-built Siberian timber company owners.

Finland felt a bit too easy and familiar for my taste, and right there I decided to make sure most of the trips I would make later were to countries where you couldn't just phone up and buy a ticket with a credit card. Even the weather was comfortable. It was 70 degrees and sunny, which has been known to happen in Britain (although not in Wales). The city was clogged with traffic. All the drivers not only had a mobile phone, they were invariably using it as they screeched their Mercedes around the harbour. As we all know, there are one or two mobile phones in use in the UK. But we're way behind the Finns. There, something like 65% of the population - not the working-age population, this is toddlers and grannies included - had a mobile before the end of 1999. Think what that will be now.

If there were any Albanians here, they were keeping a low profile. They aren't obviously a great travelling nation, it would be fair to say, but I'd expected to see one or two in Helsinki's central squares. I'd not had much success when I tried to find out a bit about their football, as there wasn't an official website for the national side, or not that I could find. I eventually found a page that listed the names of their current squad. You could click on the names, but all the extra information you got was the player's date of birth and maybe their club. Thus Igli Tare was born on 25 July 1973 and played for Kaiserslautern. Another link was to a records page, which listed one Fotis Strakosha as the country's most capped player, with 31 appearances.

I wasn't the only one struggling for information. This site listed Albania's top international goalscorer as 'Unknown Player'. Going by this website, this shadowy Gary Lineker of the Adriatic had found the net a staggering six times for his country without anyone bothering to make a note of what his name was. If you clicked on the link at 'Unknown Player' you got taken, logically enough I suppose, to an entirely blank page, presumably in readiness for when someone works out who it actually was who'd tucked away all those poacher's goals.

Finnish football is a bit more mainstream, but not by much. Players like Litmanen and Hyypia may represent the country at the top level of the European club scene, but crowds in the domestic league are disappointingly low - no more than a couple of thousand, even for Helsinki derbies. The fact that, until recently, these derbies were played in the Olympic Stadium, capacity 40,000 or so, meant that the atmosphere at these games was probably about as motivational for the players as Glamorgan batting for a draw on a damp Tuesday in Abergavenny.

The Finns didn't seem to have any confidence that they could get behind their team. The next home game after Albania was against Kevin Keegan's (or so they thought at the time) England side. Not many England fans will need reminding of England's abysmal performance under Kevin Keegan in the Euro 2000 finals, just over three months before their trip to Helsinki, but the Finns weren't going to buy any gung-ho 'let's get England while they're down, we can lift our boys to the performance of their life' kind of thinking. Instead, the fans I spoke to before and after the Albania game said they'd better get to the Olympic Stadium early on

October 11, because England would go two up in ten minutes and that would be that - the game would be lost by then, they said, and any atmosphere created would vanish just as quickly.

The Finnish FA had made a shrewd move for the Albania game. Figuring, probably rightly, that the match was unlikely to threaten the attendance record at the Olympic Stadium, they moved it to the catchily named Toolon Jalkapallostadion, thankfully also known as the Finnair Stadium, newly-built alongside the much bigger Olympic stadium. With a capacity of just under 11,000, there was a good chance the place would be full. It was the first international game to be played at the new venue, which had only been opened the previous June. It would be shared by two of Helsinki's top clubs: HJK, who had beaten Liverpool in the home leg of an early 1980s European Cup tie, and an odd-sounding bunch called FC Jokerit who clearly relied for their success on the opposition thinking they were a laugh, or maybe turning up expecting to be involved in card games.

Kick-off was 3pm. The ground was only half a mile or so from my hotel so I walked, armed with a hot dog bought from a van on the way. The quickest way was through a park of silver birch trees and tall pines. Cyclists rode by me in no great hurry. Kids out with their parents played happily among the trees. Joggers jogged and dogs were walked. Finland were about to begin their World Cup campaign, in a group that gave them a pretty good chance of getting through, given the state of German and English football at the time, but 300 yards from the ground, I hadn't yet seen anyone who looked as if they were on their way to the match.

Football comes a long way behind some other sports in Finland. Normally it's ice-hockey that dominates the back pages, but this weekend the counter-attraction was the Finland-Sweden athletics meeting taking place in the adjoining Olympic Stadium that evening and the one after. The only reason the football was at 3pm was to avoid clashing with the athletics, which kind of put the football in perspective. Imagine England moving a Wembley World Cup game to QPR's ground, and changing the kick-off time to avoid a clash with, say, an England-Scotland athletics meeting, and you'll have some idea of how far down the pecking order football comes in Finland. In the stadium complex, a dozen or more marquees had been put up by the sponsors of the athletics meeting. Half of them were selling mobile phones.

About 2pm there couldn't have been more than a few hundred people at the ground. When they're empty, places like stadiums can seem pretty soulless, the more so if they're modern and made out of only two things - concrete and plastic bucket seats. This one was no exception. Despite the superb weather, the build-up to the game was low-key in the extreme. Everyone clearly felt that as they had a reserved seat anyway, what was the point of arriving early? Arriving at ten to three still gave them time to find their seat, buy a coke and a hot dog, eat it and still be in time to stand for the National Anthems (Albania's and Finland's are both mercifully short).

Around 2.30 Albania came out and flounced across the pitch a few times, doing not terribly fearsome-looking arms-like-windmills warmup exercises. Then the coach got them jogging along slowly and then suddenly raising one leg bent at the knee. One two three four, hup! One two three four, hup! If players knew the half of how ridiculous they looked doing these kinds of exercises, they wouldn't bother.

About a quarter to three the ground at last began to look as if people had turned up expecting something to happen. The public address announced the names of both sides' starting line-ups. My chum from the Albania web pages, Igli Tare of Kaiserslautern, was in the number 11 shirt, and it looked like goalkeeper Froto Strakosha was about to extend his appearances record. All the Albanian players and substitutes appeared to have names, so we wouldn't be seeing the country's mystery all-time Golden Boot winner. Finland's overseas-based players got the biggest cheers, and those based in that footballing mecca - yes, the UK - got the biggest cheers of all, even if they were a goalkeeper for Dundee United.

However, it was skipper and Finnish footballing legend, Jari Litmanen, who got the biggest roar of the day, at least until he earned an even louder one by scoring from a free kick just on half-time. Litmanen has been around a fair while now. He was on

YOU COME WITH ME - I GET TICKETS

Barcelona's books at this stage, before his move to Liverpool, and on the evidence of this game he was playing as well as ever. He was the first player to put the country's game on the map, by replacing Dennis Bergkamp, no less, at Ajax Amsterdam, helping them to a Champions' League title in 1995, and rejoining them from Anfield late in 2002. Sami Hyypia of Liverpool, and rising UK-based talent like Jonatan Johansson and Mikael Forssell, were acclaimed as superstars. Relatively speaking. The whole crowd was still pretty muted, apart from a few shouts of 'Suomi! ('Finland!') and a few yelping, enthusiastic kids with blue and white face paint sitting next to their mums and dads.

The whole occasion was beginning to resemble a trip to the cinema. You turned up with the whole family five or ten minutes before the start, expecting an hour and a half to two hours' entertainment, with an intermission halfway through. I was in the equivalent of the one and nines, two rows from the front. You couldn't buy, or bring, alcohol (sensibly enough, as Finns tend to bypass beer and go straight to vodka, which they drink as if it was beer. I'll spare you the stats but the country's per capita consumption of the heavier types of alcohol is phenomenal). Instead, all you could get to drink here was coca cola or other fizzy cold drinks. The food was straight out of your local Odeon/Warner multiplex: hot dogs, chocolate bars, bags of nuts and, the proof of this analogy for me, huge cartons of popcorn. There wasn't a Pukka Balti Pie or plastic lager glass in sight. But at half-time people really did appear with trays round their necks and stood at the front selling chocolate bars and ice-creams. I was careful not to unwrap a sweet in case I rustled the wrapper.

At last we got under way. The Albanian players weren't the biggest but they had excellent pace, getting behind the Finnish defence on several occasions. One of their defenders made frequent incursions down the right, but got sworn at by his team mates for fluffing potential scoring chances once he'd done the hard bit. But the Finns had most of the play and Litmanen's unstoppable shot put them one up at the break. 'Hyvaa', a few of the Finns around me muttered quietly. 'Hyvaa' means good, and was high praise.

WHAT PRICE YOU WANT TO PAY?

Albania pulled one back about 20 minutes into the second half when Edvin Murati scored, only to go off injured a few minutes later. The Finns had to make some substitutions too and Riihilahti, who had only been on for a handful of minutes, slotted home a loose ball after a corner. There were still over 20 minutes to go, and very soon afterwards the Finns made life difficult for themselves. Janne Saarinen, playing on what was now his home ground, got himself sent off for two bookable offences, the first being for a dive. As for the offence that got him the red card, call me Arsene Wenger if you must, but even though I was five yards from the touchline with a perfect view right on halfway, I didn't see the incident. But actually it didn't cause the home team much bother and they held on pretty comfortably until the end. Later it turned out that Saarinen had gone off for a 'physical challenge on an Albanian defender'.

In the Willem K bar afterwards, the queue was out the door. An orderly queue for beer. In the UK we expect the bar staff to know who got there in roughly what order, but in Finland they spare them the embarrassment of getting it wrong by assembling in a perfectly formed queue with only one person at the bar at any one time. When you get to the front, you buy a drink for yourself and let the people with you sort themselves out. There is no concept of buying a round. Of course, with beer at over £3 for less than a pint, this apparent selfishness is totally understandable. After stopping off at the cashpoint first, I joined the queue, and started talking to some of the fans.

'We were lucky,' said one. 'That was not our best game.'

'We played far better against Norway in the summer,' another one told me. 'But that was a friendly, so it doesn't really count.' But clearly they were proud of that win over Norway, and Finland's good performances in the qualifiers for Euro 2000 had also contributed to raised expectations for today's game - if not, at the time, for the game against England a month later.

I asked them what they thought of the sending off. 'The referee made some funny decisions,' they all said more or less in unison. In between calls on their mobiles, a couple of them explained how and why Finland had never been to the finals of a major tournament. One would start the story, and the other would pick it up when the first one's mobile rang. Then he would suddenly have to answer his own phone and the first one would resume. I began to feel like the parcel at a childrens' party. When I could get their attention off their phones, I tried them with the theory that this was their best opportunity ever to get to a major tournament, with the country's football on the rise and their Group 9 rivals Germany and England a long way from their best. Albania they'd just seen off, and Greece was, well, Greece. This was the opposite of a Group of Death, right now this looked like a Group of Has-Beens-And-Won't-Be-Again-For-A-Whiles. Someone had to win it. I think they agreed but didn't want to seem too confident - a feeling well known to many an underdog who can see maybe a glimmer of a real chance.

When his phone battery had run out, one of them told me about a kind of north-south divide in Finnish football. The south of Finland is more or less OK for weather - reliably warm summers, constant daylight for weeks in June/July and, in winter, nothing too much worse than in central Europe, except maybe the lack of daylight. And there's always the vodka to help you through that, as many Finns have discovered to their cost.

But up in the north it's a different story. Weeks of constant darkness, annually migrating reindeer and metres-deep snow and ice make maintaining a natural grass pitch something of a challenge. Yet Rovaniemi, a town on the Arctic Circle, has a top division football team. Rovaniemi is also the official residence of someone even better known than these (inevitably nicknamed) 'Brazilians of the Tundra'. Rovaniemi is home to Father Christmas. However, Santa is clearly not a football fan. If he was, you'd have thought he would have answered the Rovaniemi manager's prayers one foggy Christmas Eve by shoving a couple of top international strikers down the relevant chimney on his way out of town. But back to the plot. All of the Finnish league's softie, mainly Helsinki-based, southerners keep hoping that Rovaniemi will get themselves relegated, because they don't like the long cold trek up there. Happily, the plucky northerners hold on each season, and were 8th out of 12 the weekend I was there.

WHAT PRICE YOU WANT TO PAY?

The Finnish league structure is labyrinthine, but at the top, one team is relegated each season. Later I looked in the paper to see who might replace this season's bottom club from the next league down - the Finnish season ends in autumn and so was drawing to a close. Whereas in England, and just about everywhere else in Europe, you can mostly tell where a team comes from because the relevant town or city helpfully figures in the club's name, this is not so in Finland. Here are just some of Finland's lower league clubs, and I promise I'm not making any of these up: HyPS, PS-44, KaaPo, LoPa (a team of high quality golfers) and, last but not least, FC Santa Claus of the northern league second division, who had held on for a 2:2 draw against neighbours FC Kiisto on the day of the Albania game. The match report said that FC Santa Claus had eleven very well-rounded players, but, owing to a lack of fitness, too many away matches in December, and a fatal tendency to play in the 4-3-2-1 Christmas Tree formation, they gave away a sackful of goals each year.

In the best Scandinavian tradition, all these fans in the Willem K knew English football inside out (and the fashion statements of its players. The hairstyle of one Premiership player, they thought, meant that he 'looks like German porno star'). I couldn't comment, not being familiar with many German porno stars. But that season an obscure Finnish pay-TV channel had bought the rights to English Premiership matches, which had reduced that league's visibility every bit as much as you would think. Nationwide League and a few FA Cup games were all the ordinary punters would get that year. But as heaps of Finns play for teams like Bolton, Charlton and Crystal Palace - none of them total strangers to life outside the Premiership - there's lots for the country's fans to cheer. To misquote rugby's Bill McLaren, there's rejoicing in the streets of Helsinki when goalkeeper Jussi Jaaskelainen's Bolton keep a clean sheet. The local weekly footy paper has three tightly-packed pages on Finnish football each week, five or so in total on all non-UK European football, and then it goes completely OTT about everything connected with the British, for which in this context read English, game. There's at least six pages every week - and this is a paper with more words on each page than in a whole week of the *Daily Mail*. There's a level of detail about teams like Gillingham and Preston you'd be unlikely to find in any English national paper. Want to know who was yellow-carded in Tranmere's 2-1 win over Stockport? Then *Veikkaaja* is the paper for you. Provided you can find it on the city's newsstands, that is, among titles (English language ones) glamourising violent death. Anyone for *Killer Handguns Gazette* ('Stop Him Dead @ 30 Metres!!') or the enduringly popular *Samurai Combat Knives Monthly*?

One of my new pals had a spare ticket to the athletics that night, so that's where I ended up. As everyone I'd spoken to had predicted, the athletics crowd was three times the size and three times as passionate as the football crowd in the afternoon. It was a warm evening and there were jazz bands and open air cafes full of people having an enviably good time. The Finns do know how to relax and enjoy themselves. It was a knowledgeable and involved crowd - a crowd of fans, rather than the mere spectators the football had been played in front of. I stayed till the third Swede had trailed in last in the 10,000 metres and then left. I was already looking forward to Sunday, and Estonia, and Luis Figo's Portugal.

3.

That's Ott.
Everyone Respects Him

Estonia - Portugal, Kadriorg Stadium, Tallinn,
3 September 2000

IT'S ONLY AN HOUR and 30 minutes by catamaran across from Helsinki to Tallinn, so I got myself a coffee and somewhere to sit just as we left, and wrote down in a notebook every single thing I knew about Estonian football. Once I'd finished doing that, I looked at my watch. Still an hour and twenty nine minutes to go before we reached Tallinn.

I looked at what I'd written. 'Tricky and often underrated'. 'Likely to pack the box'. And finally, something that looked very like, 'the plucky Baltic outfit will pack nine or ten in the box, but today's visitors will be looking to come away with all three points from this one'. As the catamaran got into gear I did remember one or two more things. In the top division of the old Soviet league, there was no club side from Estonia, whereas just about all the other former Soviet republics had at least one team. Mart Poom, between the sticks for Derby County at the time, was their most famous name by a distance. And that August, in the first World Cup 2002 qualifying game played in a European group, Estonia had beaten Andorra and so, artificially of course, they were top of the heap, ahead of Portugal, the Netherlands and Ireland.

On one occasion a few years previously, when Estonia didn't show up for the game, Scotland had been the 'only team in Tallinn', but in fact they were wrong: there was at least one more team in

YOU COME WITH ME - I GET TICKETS

Tallinn, a club side rejoicing in the name of Flora. I scratched my head. That was as far as my knowledge went. But I was looking forward to this one. Tallinn was a great city. And I would be seeing Luis Figo for the price of the catamaran cafeteria's tea.

This game was attracting massive interest locally. The Portuguese team were reportedly amazed to find 300 fans waiting for them at the airport, not expecting to find anything like that level of interest in what they maybe sub-consciously assumed was a footballing backwater. Only a few weeks before, Luis Figo had moved from Barcelona to Real Madrid for £37 million, a world record. Yet here he was showing his passport at Tallinn airport. £37 million, at 25 Estonian crowns to the pound, comes out at just under one billion crowns. Even in the fabulously wealthy footballing nations of Western Europe, that amount of money for a footballer was considered outrageous. In a country of low incomes and a struggling economy, deals of this kind were from another planet.

Portugal were picking things up after a highly controversial exit from Euro 2000. In their semi-final against France, they had had a last-minute penalty awarded against them for a handball felt to be accidental by all the Portuguese and by a fair few neutrals as well. Zinedine Zidane did the rest from the penalty spot and that was the last kick of the game. Portugal were out, and they weren't happy. Several of them surrounded the referee, tempers flared and the ref was jostled and generally roughed up. By any standards the incident at Euro 2000 was bad and lengthy bans were handed out to at least three of the Portuguese players - bans that would take effect today, as the Portuguese hadn't kicked (or handled) a ball competitively since then. But the main reason for the interest this game was generating was quite simply that Portugal were a quality side; a side that had won plaudits from all quarters for their play in Euro 2000, when England, Romania, and especially Germany were swept aside by inventive and incisive football. These were the superstars being driven away to Tallinn's Olympia hotel.

I had to make do with a coffee in the main square until it was time to meet Martin. Martin was a student in Tartu, Estonia's main university town, and a regular in the main Estonian supporters' association. He was coming to Tallinn by bus with, I hoped, two tickets for the game.

The vanguard of the Scottish contingent had made it back to Tallinn from their victory over Latvia the day before, and had taken over the terraces of a couple of bars along one side of the square. Somehow I didn't feel ready for tired and probably badly hungover Celtic fans, so I got my coffee from another bar, and then something to eat in one of the amazing vaulted medieval cellar restaurants in the old town. When I came out, the weather had turned foul.

I'd arranged to meet Martin in the Vana Villemi bar a couple of hours before the 5pm kick off. I thought this would be about half an hour's walk from my hotel, but that was reckoning without the rain and my ability to get lost. After the allotted 30 minutes, I was feeling wet and fed up and thus failed to notice that I had walked past the bar Martin had said I couldn't miss. So, being English, and lost, I did what English people do in this situation and found a policeman to ask the way. The constable was on an extended vodka and fag break at the back entrance of the police station (that's how lost I was) and was just about sober enough to tell me to ask someone else inside. This was good advice, as his sidekick was 20 years younger and alcohol hadn't yet damaged him quite so badly.

Luckily the Vana Villemi, when I eventually found it, was just the kind of place everyone wants to find when they're as soaked as I was. It was warm, dry and friendly; a cross between an English pub and a Wild West saloon, with a bare wooden floor, ample good food and beer and not a tourist in sight. Martin was already there. Although he had a Russian surname, he was clearly passionate about Estonia as a country and its football in particular. We got a beer and started to talk about the state of the domestic game.

'Well, the crowds in the Estonian league are pretty small,' he said, 'maybe 100 people.'

'Only 100?' I said. In Finland I'd been told even Helsinki derby games attracted just 2,000 people and no atmosphere, but 100 was fewer than Forest Green Rovers got on a wet Friday night in January. I queried it. 'How come it's so few?'

YOU COME WITH ME - I GET TICKETS

'Because all the stars play abroad. We only ever see them when they play at home for the national side.'

'So don't you think your top players should play in the Estonian league, so as to encourage greater interest and to get people here into the habit of going to watch them?'

Martin was very definite about this. 'No,' he said firmly, 'the only way they will build up international expertise and experience is by playing abroad. There they can learn from other coaches, other styles of play and bring all that home to Estonia.'

That was the theory, anyway. He was very pleased with the way so many of the country's Under-21 players had developed. Several of them had played in the Under-21 game the day before and would turn out again in the game today, at least as substitutes. 'Shouldn't you have beaten Andorra by more?' I asked him, referring to Estonia's victorious start to this campaign. 1-0 with a second half penalty was not exactly a crushing of the men from the Pyrenees.

'What can you do,' he asked, 'when they play 11 men in the box?' Then he smiled and admitted that Estonia would do exactly the same against Portugal today. All 11, huh? On the catamaran that morning I'd guessed it would be only 9 or 10. Showed how much I knew about Estonian football.

Gradually it became obvious how many people Martin knew in the Estonian football set-up. The bar began to fill up with people he recognised, all wearing Estonian replica kits. If all Martin's friends showed up at Estonian league games, they'd double the crowd. An hour before kick off, and in no great hurry, Martin picked up the large bag he had with him and we set off for Kadriorg stadium. Martin was pleasantly surprised to see people heading for the stadium from all sides and told me how he had resisted the temptation to exploit the black market for tickets - a black market reputedly selling tickets for 10 times more than their £4 face value - and that was to locals, as there were very few Portuguese around. Never before had there been such demand for tickets for a game in Estonia.

'Get ready for the most pathetic stadium in the world,' said Martin as we turned a corner, just in case I was expecting another Stade de France. But it wasn't pathetic at all. It may be a touch run-down and, like so many stadiums outside the UK, it has the same kind of irritating running track all round the pitch that you can never envisage anyone using and which serves only to make everybody's view of the game more distant. But the atmosphere inside was what counted, and made this game a much more memorable one than the Finland one I'd seen the day before. Martin said that a new stadium, with a much larger capacity (up to 15,000), was being built not far away.

After ostentatiously collecting his tickets from the 'VIP collection point' - a small white wooden hut by the front gate - Martin led me to the back row of the terrace near the halfway line, and for the first time I discovered what was in Martin's bag. No one around us showed any surprise when he produced and distributed an assortment of rattles, whistles, horns, mini trumpets, and a giant Estonian flag complete with scissors and parcel tape to stick it over the advertising hoardings. It was almost as if it was Martin's job to bring the musical instruments, while it was up to another person to supply, say, the beer and pretzels and someone else's job to bring scarves and hats for the whole gang. Around us some of the hardcore Estonian support was getting in the mood in a way the Finns never did the day before. 'Eesti! Eesti! (Estonia!)', sang the self-appointed cheerleaders, a bit hairier and spottier than Miami Dolphins cheerleaders, and masculine to boot, but you can't have everything, and the crowd dutifully responded. 'Roadsweeper', one of Martin's chums from the bar, was there with a mobile phone clamped to his ear. He looked like something out of the Soviet 'Spetsnaz' Special Forces in his combat trousers, and was one of the noisiest, but if there was a ringleader, it was an even taller lad in his early thirties, wearing what looked like a faded Soviet-era Zhalgiris Vilnius baseball cap, sawn-off jeans and of course the apparently mandatory Estonian replica kit top. I asked Martin who he was.

'That's Ott,' he replied, 'he's one of the oldest, everyone respects him.' This was pretty good, I thought, for a bloke who looked like your standard terraces hard man, but he probably helped old ladies on and off buses when there wasn't an Estonia home game to go to.

Not only had Martin seen just about every game played by Estonia in their 10-year post-Soviet history, both home and away, but so had most of this part of the crowd. Even though he lived in Tartu, Martin evidently recognised nearly all the faces around us and was busily finalising the details of the group's forthcoming trip to Andorra and Ireland in mid-October for Estonia's next games, while simultaneously handing out various low-budget plastic musical instruments to all and sundry. Their group's Andorra trip was to be by road, which must have taken a fair bit of planning.

'Eesti, suru Portugal vastu muru!' yelled Ott and everyone else around me, urging their team to 'push Portugal against the grass', which probably ranks alongside 'Korea Team Fighting' as one of the more naff football chants. When national anthem time came round I sort of mumbled and tried to look as if I belonged there, a bit like John Redwood at the Welsh Tory Party conference. Actually it probably looked as if I did belong there, as Martin, already wearing an Estonian top, just happened to have found another one at the bottom once all his tin whistles had been handed out. He gave this one to me to wear. 'Eesti Jalgpalli Litt' said the logo on my chest.

The game got going. Early on, Estonia had quite a few chances, and created as many openings as the Portuguese. Urmas Rooba, their left back, took the ball off Figo several times, raising the roof every time he did so. At the back, goalkeeper Mart Poom has Beckham-style superstar status in Estonia. Whenever he made a save, of even the most routine kind, up went a shout of 'Jaa!! Mart!!' The young lad in front of me, wearing an Aston Villa shirt, laid into Figo with some choice language doubtless picked up from English supporters on TV. It was an odd mixture from this crowd. They weren't sure whether to be awe-struck at the sight of these world class players performing on their own patch (the right word for some bits of this playing area) or whether to yell abuse at them. Mostly they settled for being awe-struck.

5pm was an unusual kick-off time, but Martin explained that this was to ensure the game was over before floodlighting would be needed. It would get dark about 7pm, so they were cutting it fairly fine. The Kadriorg stadium has no floodlights, and this was the root cause of the problem a few years ago when Estonia didn't show up for the game with Scotland. The two teams had wanted the game played at different times, UEFA got involved, both sides thought the matter had been resolved but evidently there was a misunderstanding, and so on and so forth. Scotland were awarded the match by default. Scotland and Estonia's footballing relations have not yet fully recovered.

Portugal scored on 13 minutes, with a long-range shot from Rui Costa. Suddenly there was silence, but the noise soon picked up again and it was still 1-0 at half time. A Beckham-style Figo free kick soon after the break extended the lead, and then Figo set up the Joao Pinto header that put it beyond any doubt. Portugal went off the boil completely in the last 15 minutes, with the game in the bag, and Estonia came back strongly with a goal 6 minutes from the end. It was now after 6.30pm and starting to get dark. 'There's still time, there's still time,' said Martin excitedly, pointing to the picture in the programme of the referee in Euro 2000 giving France the dodgy penalty that led to Portugal's defeat and elimination. 'Now we need this referee! He can win it for us!' The last 6 minutes saw Estonia bombard the goal of the Portuguese superstars incessantly, creating several good chances that could, maybe should, have gone in. If Estonia could have brought it back to 3-2, even with only a minute left, the place would have erupted, and that's not bad for a crowd of under 5,000. But sadly it didn't happen. Still, the goal was evident consolation, and the long periods of play where the Estonians matched their opponents meant the crowd went home with honour satisfied. 3-1 to Portugal.

There weren't many Portuguese fans at the game, only 20 or so, but then Estonia is about as far away from Lisbon as it's possible to get in Europe. The ones who were there turned out to be based in Sweden or Finland and had travelled to Estonia for the game because it was relatively close. One of them told me that the Portuguese coaching staff were mighty unhappy with the way Portugal had let the Estonians come back and dominate the last part of the game, when in all honesty they could have pressed on and scored six. Portuguese boss Antonio Oliveira claimed his side weren't yet in 'top physical condition'. Another of the Portuguese fans told me afterwards that their goalkeeping coach had used a single, fairly brief word to describe his team's performance in the last 15 minutes when Estonia came back so strongly.

Martin and his group were used to going round behind the main stand afterwards and even getting in to meet the players. He'd been confident that we would be able to do the same after this match, so off we went, but as this was such a huge game for Estonia, some extremely burly security lads were out in considerable numbers and there was no chance of getting anywhere near the door, or even seeing anything much past the shaven heads of the Enforcement Division of the Estonian FA. Between the skulls you could occasionally glimpse players of both sides coming out, mostly talking into a mobile phone, and sometimes giving a brief, distracted wave as they got on their bus. The driver of the Portuguese bus switched on the engine and cleared off and that was that really. The team flew out of Estonia that night. You had to wonder whether the Portuguese side felt that Estonia was a big enough stage for them and worthy of 90 minutes' full effort, because there was a trace of let's-get-the-job-done-and-get-out-of-here in their attitude. As for the home fans, the overwhelming feeling at this game was the enthusiasm of every Estonian there, even Russian-speaking Estonians, all desperately keen to enjoy their moment in the reflected limelight of the visit by one of Europe's top teams. For them, home games against real quality national sides only happen about once, maybe twice a year (and not at all at club level), so the locals were going to make sure they milked the occasion.

Martin, his friends and I talked a bit more to the Portuguese supporters, including a lad called Fernando, who had been a lecturer at Portsmouth Polytechnic in the early 1990s and was now working in Sweden. He and his wife had arrived in Tallinn that day. They were enthusiastic about being there, and everyone took everyone's photo and shook hands on a good game in a way that was perfectly genuine, and which you can largely forget about in many countries, where football has undergone Bill Shankly's sometimes regrettable 'more-important-than-life-or-death' transformation.

Win, lose or draw, for Martin and his gang, it was back to the Vana Villemi afterwards. Ivar, who was at the table with us and who'd just bought a round, told me he was a referee in the Estonian second and third divisions. With crowds of 100 in the top division, I decided not to ask him what the gate for those games was (probably a piece of string across a muddy lane). His chum Vitor, from Lisbon, told me he'd been working in Hammeenlinna, a Finnish town about 100 miles from Helsinki, for 11 years now, and that he'd met Ivar at an ice-hockey match there six months before. As ice hockey isn't big in Portugal, he'd arranged to meet up with Ivar again for the football when the Portuguese came to Tallinn.

'Roadsweeper' went off home with his wife, who worked behind the bar, at about 9.30. Ivar and another ref chum of his had also gone, and Martin was about to leave to catch the final bus back to Tartu. The Vana Villemi was emptying fast, so after a final photo session and more explanations of what exactly I was doing there, I walked back to my hotel. Instead of looking at me suspiciously as if I was a logo short of a replica kit top, which I undoubtedly felt like sometimes in these places, they seemed quite chuffed that out of all the countries I could have chosen to go to, I had decided to come to their neck of the woods.

In the morning I had a couple of hours to spare before the boat left so I headed back to the Old Town. The Latvia-bound Scots I'd met on the way to Finland had planned on going to the Estonia game on their way home, but as the match was a sell-out I saw only one kilt at the Kadriorg, and even that was a photo in the newspaper the day after the game. Instead, quite a few of the Scots were here, in the bars of the Old Town Square and looking distinctly jet-lagged.

There were more Scots at the harbour, mainly Rangers fans, judging by what they were wearing. Celtic fans seemed to have preferred the main square. The Ibrox crowd were, as expected, to be found in the bar, but they were played out, drinking as if going through the motions. By the time they'd found the bar on the catamaran back to Helsinki, they were asleep. Or maybe the in-house TV programming had finished them off. In between on-board video cam shots of all the spray and stuff coming out of the back, we were shown tourist trailers for Tallinn (the place everybody had in fact just come from, but I'm sure the schedulers knew what they were doing), interspersed with a thankfully inaudible American cop series with Estonian subtitles. I ate a slice of cold, soggy pizza and tried to make out what I could of newspaper reports of yesterday's game.

I'd bought two Estonian newspapers, one in Russian (imaginatively titled *Estonia*) and one in Estonian. The Estonian language paper had got its act together overnight - a 5pm kick off in the capital doesn't present too many print deadlines, not when it's clearly the main event - with page after page of coverage, but the Russian one just had a human interest piece on the front page and told its readers to wait for the next issue if they actually wanted to know the result or read a report on the match. The article didn't know whether to take a slightly superior, avuncular 'gosh, aren't these soccer fans a jolly bunch of ruffians' line, or whether to be as enthusiastic about the Portuguese visit as everyone else was. 'Figo's Euro 2000 performances make him a rival to Zidane as the Best Footballer in the World', purred the writer, only to then call Figo's $56 million move to Real a 'scandal' and have a pop at the Estonian fans for their underhand efforts to get in and see the game, which had required the police to be 'vigilant', as he put it. He seemed surprised that the stadium was full with all tickets sold out.

For the result and a match report you had to turn to the opinion-forming Estonian organ, *Postimees*, whose sports staff had come up trumps. Unfortunately I couldn't understand a word of *Postimees*' exhaustive coverage. Estonian words are all about 19 letters long, but at least the prominently displayed 3-1 result and numerous pictures of Figo showed I was looking at the right part of the paper. There was a panel at the bottom of one page with assessments and marks out of ten for each player's performance. Here's what they had to say about the tough-tackling Urmas Rooba, who'd cleanly dispossessed Figo several times in the game. 'Taani meistrisarjas mangimine on margatavalt enesekindlust lisanud'. I don't think anyone could argue with that.

4.

Widzew Hool's

Poland - Belarus, Widzew Stadium, Lodz, Saturday 7 October 2000

MARCIN HAD TOLD ME I had to meet Slavomir to collect my ticket. When I rang Slavomir from Warsaw airport, he told me that he drove a black BMW and would be wearing black shades. I guess pink pyjamas were always going to be unlikely for someone called Slavomir.

Neither the flash wheels nor the shades seemed particularly necessary, as we'd be meeting on a walkway in the lower level of Warsaw's Central Railway Station, where he was unlikely to be able to bring his car, even if it was a BMW. And the light and UV readings probably wouldn't be excessive down there, not in October anyway. But style in the new Eastern Europe is style, and black says a lot about you, or so most Polish men under 30 seemed to think. At least, if things got nasty, I knew he probably wouldn't be able to see me.

But nothing would get nasty, because Slavomir was a Mr Fix-it for the Polish FA's official fan club, and a friend of Marcin, who I'd contacted about a ticket for Saturday's game. He was on time, which was good as my train was due to leave in ten minutes. Although the game was in Lodz, I was a day or two early, so I had time to head for Gdansk to get Marcin's thoughts about Polish football. Slavomir said that he was going to the game too, so we agreed we'd look out for each other once we got to Lodz.

YOU COME WITH ME - I GET TICKETS

Poland, like Germany, but unlike England unless Wembley's being demolished, play internationals in several of the country's major cities. This time it was Lodz's turn. Lodz is an industrial city, two hours west of Warsaw by train, and can't by any stretch of the imagination be described as glamorous or fashionable. But there's tennis, if you want glamour and fashion.

The opposition was Belarus, which handily meant I could forget about going to Belarus itself without feeling I'd wimped out of a difficult trip. With Serbia's Milosevic out of the picture, Lukashenka of Belarus remains Europe's last 'Soviet-style strongman', as tabloid jargon has it. This gross over-simplification is totally accurate. In Minsk today you can find a Dzerzhinsky Street, a Soviet Street, a Revolution Street, an Engels Street, the leafy, suburban-sounding Tank Street, a British Embassy at no. 37 Karl Marx Street, and the attractive 'October Revolution Tractor Plant no.9 Tool Makers' Association Hostel of Comrades' for anyone who feels like staying in town for a while.

Many of the new, or restored, East European footballing nations have found that their territories or populations are too small to allow more than one club side of any strength to emerge. When the Soviet Union broke up, many of the stalwarts of the former Soviet league found themselves marooned in their own countries with few domestic challengers - this was true, for example, of Dinamos Kiev and Tbilisi, Neftchi Baku, Ararat Yerevan, and Dinamo Minsk among others. Some of these sides have since fallen on hard times as Communist political favours were withdrawn, but truly strong domestic competition has not arisen. The capital city of one of the 'new' countries might produce a team that can hold its own in the early rounds of European club competitions, but that's as far as it goes.

Poland doesn't have these difficulties so acutely. For a country as ethnically and linguistically uniform as Poland, some pretty fierce footballing rivalries exist, almost English in their intensity. A crucial point is that Polish footballing power does not all rest with one club, or one city (unlike Russia, where Moscow is home to five of the 16 top division clubs), or even one region. There are at least three major footballing hotbeds - Warsaw, the Krakow-Katowice area, and Lodz itself. Although the riot police in these places may disagree, the diversity this creates can only be healthy for the nation's club game. A recent Warsaw derby between Polonia and Legia was ordered to be held behind closed doors as neither set of fans could be trusted not to trash first the place and then each other. As for the two Lodz teams, Widzew and LKS, no amount of venom is too much, and every game is an opportunity to further the rivalry - including Polish international fixtures, as I was about to see. Football matters to the fans in Lodz, and the city has known success (between them, the two Lodz clubs dominated the championship in the second half of the 1990s), but it has engendered one of the sport's more bitter hatreds.

Widzew Lodz played Manchester United in a Cup Winners' Cup first round tie in 1981. I saw the game on TV and I remember it for one of the most explosive starts to a game I've ever seen - after just 6 minutes it was 1-1. Sadly the last 84 minutes packed only half as much action into them as the first six, and 1-1 it remained, but those six minutes rooted Lodz firmly into my footballing consciousness.

Marcin met me off the train in Gdansk. He was in his early 20s and an IT student, with a couple of websites featuring stadiums around Europe, and, like most Poles of his age, he had a David Beckham-style crew cut. We went off in search of a drink. The current Polish squad were the most successful for a generation, and I asked Marcin who stood out for him.

'Watch out for Jerzy Dudek. He's one of the best keepers in Europe.' This was well before Dudek's move to Anfield to replace Sander Westerveld. Martin in Estonia had said much the same thing about Mart Poom, although Poom isn't quite in Dudek's class as a goalkeeper, or maybe that's just the way it seems, given the defences Poom has had to rely on for Estonia, Derby and Sunderland.

'Dudek is class,' Marcin went on, 'but the big name right now is Emmanuel Olisadebe. Definitely.'

I'd heard of Olisadebe - in fact I remembered well that he'd scored two goals in Poland's 3-1 demolition of Ukraine a month before. Olisadebe's name stood out somewhat as being less than typically Polish. Currently he was averaging a goal a game for Poland. Admittedly, that was after just two games. But it was to be a scoring ratio he would more or less maintain over the 18 months to come - only for him to disappoint badly in Poland's group games in the finals in Korea, where he didn't score until Poland had been eliminated.

'How come a Nigerian's playing for Poland?' It seemed a fair question to ask.

Marcin looked a bit embarrassed. 'Kwasniewski - our Prime Minister - gave him early citizenship to allow him to play. And it looks as if FIFA and UEFA are happy. At club level, both Ruch Chorzow and Wisla Krakow overlooked him, or released him after a trial, but now he's with Polonia Warsaw. They got him for $150,000. Currently he's worth $4m, which is the highest value ever for a Polish player.' I'd already heard rumours that Olisadebe could be on his way to Serie A. In fact, within 24 hours, the word was that Olisadebe had signed for Roma, subject to a medical, for as much as $7m. In the event, however, that deal didn't go through, and he went to play his club football for Panathinaikos. He nearly ended up at Birmingham, of all places, for the 2002-03 season, which goes to show what a World Cup he must have had.

Judging from some of the graffiti and skinhead haircuts I'd seen so far, I wondered what sort of reception Olisadebe got from the average tattooed and follically-challenged nineteen-year-old on the terraces at Legia Warsaw, or wherever. Marcin had no doubts.

'It's great. They love him. So long as he goes on scoring a goal a game for Poland'. Marcin was laughing as he said this. But clearly Olisadebe was flavour of the month. There was a precedent, of sorts, in the form of Ernest Wilimowski, who played for Poland in the years just before WWII, scoring 21 goals in 22 games. Then the war came, and Wilimowski agreed, or was made, to play for the Germans after 1939. Besides Sylvester Stallone and the rest of the *Escape to Victory* cast, I couldn't think who the Germans would have played against during WWII, but apparently they played a few games against teams of Croatian fascists and other teams from the Axis countries. No great surprise then that Wilimowski was not accorded the very greatest of fanfares when he returned to what was left of Poland in 1945. Nor did time heal the wounds. He died quite recently, in 1997, and despite his heroic exploits before the war, his death was not widely marked.

The Belarus game didn't seem to be a crunch game for the Poles, according to Marcin. Belarus didn't seem to be that worked up about it either. Only 100 fans were expected to make what was, after all, the country next door. It was an important World Cup qualifier, certainly, but it didn't stir Polish blood in anything like the way a game against England would. There was a recent time when, as long-suffering England fans will know, England seemed to be drawn against Poland more often than any other country, apart maybe from a period ten years ago or so when every other game was against Turkey. For the 2006 World Cup, yes, it's Poland again.

'Games against England are huge for us. Ever since Tomaszewski in 1973-4.' Ah yes, Jan Tomaszewski, Brian Clough's 'clown' of a goalkeeper who kept England out almost on his own in that Wembley game. Marcin thought Tomaszewski actually did look like a clown, but only because of that attractive mid-70s hairstyle he had, a kind of state-owned Keeganesque bubble perm. Poland's victory over England in that campaign remains the country's only win against the English. It was a huge moment in the country's footballing history. The Poles call the spirit they showed in that game 'oborona Czestochowa' - Czestochowa is one of the most revered Catholic shrines in Poland, while 'oborona' means 'defence', and for Poles the phrase calls to mind heroic, almost miraculous exploits to deny a foreign foe. Military terminology is used too often in football, but in this case it was an occasion of such national significance that the language can become appropriate.

On the train to Lodz the next morning I had a go at reading a Polish weekly football magazine on the train. Unlike Scandinavia, Poland gets into its domestic football in a serious way and so most of the magazine was devoted to the domestic scene. England and Germany got a page each and, gratifyingly, France, Spain, Italy, Turkey, the Netherlands, Belgium and Portugal all had to share two pages between them. This week there was page after page of post mortem from Poland's clash with Ukraine in September, and plenty of build up to Poland's two forthcoming qualifiers: Wales were next up, in Warsaw the following Wednesday. 'First Shevchenko, now Giggs', said the magazine, its editors clearly chuffed to bits that two such big names would be taking on the national team in such quick succession.

When listing international teams, newspapers everywhere often print the clubs the players belong to, even when neither player nor club is particularly famous. So the club affiliations of all the Welsh squad were listed. What is it about the names of British clubs that gets so mangled in what isn't even translation? Dean Saunders was down, correctly for the time, as playing for Bradford City. Ditto Nathan Blake for Blackburn Rovers. But Darren Ward was not so lucky, being listed as a 'Notts County Nottingham' player. Gareth Roberts had apparently signed for a club called 'Tranmere Rovers Birkenhead' and, worst of the lot, Mark Pembridge for 'Everton Liverpool'. So often, non-English speakers talk about 'Celtic Glasgow' and 'FC Arsenal London', and I want to whack them over the head and say no, listen, it's Glasgow Celtic, if you really must add the city. And it's just Arsenal. We don't do this to their names, do we? No one talks about 'Munich Bayern' or 'Milan Inter'. We all know Lazio is a Rome club, so we don't add on the city name. To be fair, though, it was us in the UK that came up with the notion of a 'Borussia Derby' between Moenchengladbach and Dortmund. Where did you say Borussia was? And then there was the time when a Liverpool official was talking about how his club had been drawn with Standard Liege in a European tournament, adding helpfully that the first leg would be in Standard.

I got off the train and walked towards the centre of Lodz. The Saturday lunchtime groups of denim-clad, crew-cut heavies hanging around on corners began to get larger and, they probably hoped, more intimidating. It seemed to be more or less obligatory to have a skinhead haircut if you were male, under 25 and interested in football.

WIDZEW HOOL'S

At first sight the city was similarly unwelcoming. The communists put a lot of heavy industry there, and the city's 19th century textile-derived prosperity has been decaying for some while. Facades were crumbling and factories had closed. An elderly couple were carefully picking out firewood for the winter from a row of large trash containers. This was the fourth Polish city I'd visited, but the first to be off the visitor trail and well away from much in the way of Western investment. Lodz is the second biggest city in the country, but it merited just five pages in my 500 page guidebook to Poland. Of those five pages, one was a map, and a second was devoted to listing all the transport options you had if, or rather when, you wanted to get away again.

It was the day of England's last game at the old Wembley, and of course the last game with Kevin Keegan as England manager. Early evening Polish TV news showed plenty of replays of the German free kick that wriggled out of Seaman's grasp. I went for a Chinese meal to cheer myself up before taking the tram out to the Widzew Lodz stadium. Outside it, even with two hours still before kick-off, you couldn't move for police riot crew. They were everywhere and looked as if they meant business. In half an hour's time it was to become obvious that they weren't wearing all that kit for fun.

You could be forgiven for concluding that the city's LKS and Widzew fans beg to differ sometimes as to which of the two teams is more deserving of support. One thirty-yard stretch of wall I'd seen from the train just outside the city, in Widzew-held territory, read as follows, verbatim from left to right: WIDZEW PRIDE OF LODZ, WIDZEW HOOL'S, DESTROYER'S, HOOLIGAN'S, WIDZEW POWER, and lampooned the initials LKS by showing the K as a Star of David. The LKS fans are probably equally broad minded and ungrammatical.

This being an international match, fans of both clubs had come along. A perfect opportunity, then, to continue the debate about the relative merits of their two football clubs. An hour or so before the game, groups of them started pinging each other with bottles and stones and charged into each other in an all-out scrap. In waded the riot squad to break it up, whereupon the two sets of rival fans forgot their differences and teamed up to have a go at the police instead, who had to fire shots in the air to get everyone to calm down. 34 people were arrested. Football hooligans' original role models may have been English, but don't let anyone tell you it's only the English that do this kind of thing. It didn't look like a good idea to hang around watching for long, and most of the time, while the bottles were flying and the batons flailing, I was round the other side of the ground completing the Polish part of my international hot-dog taste comparison test (I wouldn't recommend it - if I were you, I'd try a Belgian one instead, or a Turkish one if you've got a strong stomach).

It was getting dark. I called Slavomir a couple of times from outside the ground, but his phone was switched off and I never saw him. Maybe his BMW had broken down on the way. Or perhaps I just didn't recognise him: it was now dark, and maybe even he'd decided the hard-man shades weren't worth it under floodlights.

So it was just me. In Finland (as I would again more or less everywhere I went), I'd found fans perfectly happy to talk to a complete stranger about their team and what they thought of that day's game, and then about football generally and anything else. Here there was rather less friendliness to outsiders. Instead, when I spoke to some fans over a beer on the terrace outside, there was a kind of bristling what's-it-to-you? aggression and a sense of unease that I hadn't encountered anywhere else so far, and which was difficult to square with Marcin's friendliness. Perhaps, like Ott in Estonia, they all just cultivated a hard image, which meant not talking to anyone you didn't know, but underneath that, they were soft as butter. To blend in, you had to wear black or dark clothes, preferably a tracksuit or shellsuit, with a Widzew, LKS or Poland scarf, and it went without saying that you had to be a skinhead. The crowd was 99% male, 99% under 30, and 100% white. The Welsh FA expressed a few concerns about possible trouble at their game in Warsaw a few days later, but in the event it passed off without incident, unlike today.

I went and found a seat. There was a 15 metre-high thick metal fence all around the pitch except for the main/VIP stand, whose occupants' larger wallets meant they could presumably be trusted and who probably thought they'd paid for an unobstructed view. The ground was not full, so everyone else was sitting high in the stands so as to see over the top of the fence.

It was fair enough I suppose, but the fans in this sector looked at me as an interloper from a distant universe, though here surprise seemed to outweigh the aggression I'd sensed at the beer stall. By now I was wearing a Polish national team T-shirt (the weather had been sunny all through my time in Poland, and now at 8pm it was still T-shirt weather) and here I was, looking for a space to sit in the Polish FA fan club sector, so when I asked people if they spoke English they were entitled to wonder what I was doing there and what I thought I was on. At least I think that's what they were saying. At times I wondered the same thing. A Polish friend in the UK (her parents are Polish) confirmed that Poles often understand at least a bit of Russian, given that they were forced to learn it in school under the communists. Many older people understand some German, also for grim historical reasons. But the history is so grim that many simply refuse to use either language, even to a person clearly neither German nor Russian. As it happened, the person next to me spoke English - I cleverly spotted that he was reading *Time Magazine* when I sat down. But after that, every time I turned towards him to ask him something, he was in a clinch with his decidedly presentable girlfriend and I didn't like to interrupt.

Just before the game the Belarus team names and shirt numbers were announced, first in Polish and then Russian, and the Russian version of this PA announcement got particularly derisively jeered by almost everyone. Just like England in the 70s, a toilet roll, soft, strong, and very long, was the accessory of choice for the more fanatical spectators. The Polish ultras (presumably missing 34 of their number, nursing baton bruises in a police van on the way to the local nick) behind Dudek's goal threw a dozen or so high over the fence and onto the field early in the game, with the apparent aim of making life as hard as possible for their own side's 'keeper. After that, they had their hands free to wave the little plastic Polish flags handed out at the turnstiles, which had the national colours on one side and an advertisement for a mobile phone company on the other. This was to become a recurrent theme - almost every game I went to after this one handed out some plastic gimmick to the home fans, mostly featuring the words of whichever national anthem it happened to be.

Besides the Andrex, the ultras had come equipped with flares, horns, bagfuls of ticker tape and a couple of slightly bigger Polish flags. Somebody in our sector had brought one of these as well. Every 25 seconds your view of the game was blocked as this huge flag got passed over everyone's head on the way down to the front or back up to where it started. The novelty wore off after a while. After 20 minutes a few lads near me just scrunched it up and stood on it, and then everyone could get on with watching the game.

100 Belarus fans sat bravely in the main stand opposite, and equally bravely waved a red and green flag when Belarus equalised at 1-1 late in the first half with probably the best goal of the game, a fantastic curling shot from about 25 yards that even the acclaimed Jerzy Dudek had no chance with. Poland's first goal came after a goalmouth scramble, which Wisla Krakow's Radoslaw Kaluzny finished off with a close-range volley. Poland retook the lead halfway though the second half and added a third with quarter of an hour to go. Kaluzny got both these goals as well, so he had a good night. Olisadebe was cheered to the echo every time he touched the ball in the first half, but was substituted late in the game. He was off the pace and may have had his mind on staying uninjured for his trip to Italy and the medical with Roma. Another big cheer greeted news of Germany's Wembley win over England. Interesting that, I thought: Germany, arguably equal with Russia as national historical enemy no.1, get the fans' vote over England, currently top national footballing 'enemy'.

3-1 seemed a fair result, and it put Poland on top of their Group after two games without a point dropped so far. Belarus played extremely well for a country with very limited resources and a limited standard of domestic football. They were quick, but also very physical - they picked up five yellow cards. The Polish players did a quaint little circular victory dance and followed this with an end-of-panto-style bow to the crowd before leaving the pitch.

The whole crowd dispersed immediately. It was still warm at 10pm so I walked the three miles back into town along the main road. Every minute or so the traffic lights would release another wave of cars racing back into Lodz with scarves, banners, and flags streaming out behind them in the finest French or Italian manner. The Poles were happy with their win and wanted everyone to know it.

Next day I was up at 4 am to get the train to Warsaw, from the station over the road from my hotel. I needn't have bothered getting up this early as the flight was delayed for seven hours 'due to hydraulic reasons', with a spare part having to be flown in from London. I had no Polish cash left, so my lunch consisted of large amounts of Toblerone bought on credit card, which was tasty; and both duty- and guilt-free.

Among the disappointed passengers was a tall Nigerian called Tony, who worked as a surgeon in Lodz and whose main reason for wanting to get to England appeared to be to find out what the UK papers were saying about the resignation of Kevin Keegan, at that stage an event less than 24 hours old. We chewed the fat over who would now take over the England job, neither of us getting even close to guessing who it would eventually be. Remembering that Emmanuel Olisadebe was from Nigeria, I asked Tony what he thought of him as a player.

'I got him into Poland, man,' he claimed. 'I know the owner of his club in Nigeria, and I said to him, you should come.' Tony claimed to know the owners of most of the major Lagos clubs, and said that he had trained with Sunday Oliseh, a star of the Nigerian squad at USA'94 and for some years afterwards. 'I was better than him when we were both 16.'

I let that one go. 'Why Poland then? If he's as good a player as he obviously is, why didn't he try his luck in a better-known league?' The obvious answer to that, now, was that he was on his way to Roma (well, Panathinaikos in the end, but they're no slouches) to play his club football, so the bright lights of the West had got their man.

Tony laughed. 'I tempted him with the girls, man. I've been in Poland for four years now, and I was originally only going to be here for six months. I learnt Polish from Polish girls.'

YOU COME WITH ME - I GET TICKETS

Again moving swiftly on, I explained that I'd been in Lodz for the Belarus match, and why. 'Did you see the game yesterday?' I asked.

'I was there. The Polish FA gave me tickets, as they are happy with me about Olisadebe. So you're writing a book? Lots of trips away from home?' He looked at me. 'You should check out the ladies, man. I bet you do.'

Suspecting that more of my thoughts reached higher than my waist than was the case with Tony, I told him I was hitched already. 'I'm getting married too', he said. 'I'm going to London now to meet my fiancee.'

'Is she English?'

'No, she's Nigerian. She's coming over with her mother for a week. They're going to go shopping. Rich Nigerians always come to London for their shopping.' He sighed. 'With any luck I might see a game at Highbury. I'm getting married next year. It scares me, man!' The wedding would be in Nigeria, and after that, he said, he'd probably knock his job in Poland on the head and move back to Nigeria.

'Olisadebe played last night with an ankle injury,' Tony went on. 'He played deliberately off the pace as he didn't want to risk aggravating it and failing his medical with Roma. But he'll play on Wednesday against Wales.' He thought that Wales would be a bigger test for Poland than Belarus, if only psychologically. Just because they were a British Isles team, Wales would bring out some of the 'let's beat England' factor in the Polish team, which is the kind of thing which I'm sure makes the Welsh feel even more gratitude towards the English.

Another hour or so went by and further infusions of Toblerone were required. By now I was onto my fourth bar of the sixpack, and it was beginning to taste as hideous as you'd expect from your fourth big bar of overwarm chocolate. At last the gate opened and down we went onto a bus to begin a leisurely tour of the outlying regions of Warsaw airport, which might have been pleasant in the autumn sunshine if we weren't already seven hours late. I was in the front row - of the economy section. Moving about the plane later on I noticed Tony in the back row, who just happened to have found himself next to the best looking girl on the aircraft. Jacket off, shades on, Tony was in his element. Through the hazy cloud of testosterone you could see his shirt was open almost to his waist, hinting at some not unimpressive pecs, if you liked that kind of thing, though they've never done much for me.

5.

Oh No. Now We Dance

Norway - Ukraine, Ullevaal Stadium, Oslo, Wednesday 11 October 2000

THEY WERE 15 DEEP around the counter in the Pele Bar, and it was still only 5.30pm. This was Oslo, and what a contrast to Helsinki. Despite the Finns' entirely justified reputation for copious alcohol consumption, all I'd been able to find to drink anywhere near the stadium in Finland six weeks previously had been some local approximation of Fanta. Things were very different here. £3.50 for half a litre of fizzy beer in a plastic cup was no disincentive to the Norwegians, or these Norwegians anyway.

The Pele Bar was underneath one corner of the Ullevaal Stadium, the supermodern complex in Oslo that was staging tonight's game against Ukraine. I'd gone in because the entrance just happened to be where I'd got to when I met a large group of Ukrainian fans wearing enormous sheepskin coats and coming towards me along a very narrow walkway. So I stepped inside to let them go by, and then I saw they'd all followed me in. So now we were 16 deep at the counter.

Tonight's game was a sell-out. However you sliced it, this was a big one for both sides. A defeat for Norway would leave them adrift near the bottom of their group, possibly even at the bottom. Winning would put them right back in contention in second place behind Poland, who would stay top of Group 5 more or less regardless of how tonight's games turned out. Meanwhile Ukraine were a point ahead of Norway going into the game, so losing tonight wouldn't have been so disastrous for them, especially as they were away from home and had secured all three points from a victory over Armenia the weekend before. A win tonight would put Ukraine up near the top and in good shape. So it was all set up nicely, provided Norway responded to the need to play positive football - they hadn't exactly set new standards of entertainment at Euro 2000. Maybe the urgent need to bag the three points at home would bring them out a bit.

I squeezed to the front and got myself a plastic cup of fizzy beer. I don't mind travelling alone, except at times like this when you have to buy a drink for yourself and it's abundantly clear to everyone that it's only yourself you're buying for. I've tried looking nonchalant and as if I've got at least three options for a hot social life later that evening, and as if this is merely a chill-out refuelling stop, but no one's really ever bought that one. This time, in fact, I'd rung round a few friends to see if they fancied seeing the game, as it only meant one night away. It was Norway, after all, and thus close to home and civilised. They'd see some very familiar, and really quite good players like Shevchenko, Tore Andre Flo, Rebrov, Iversen, and Solskjaer, I tried to explain.

But even with Norway I didn't get any takers. So far, everyone had chickened out of going anywhere remotely difficult - Finland didn't qualify as difficult but somehow Estonia did, and that's where I went directly from Helsinki. Lodz in Poland scored so highly on the 'Armpits of Europe' league that I was on a loser there from the start when it came to travelling with a friend. And when I tried explaining how the next one after Norway could end up being somewhere like Romania or Russia, and did they want to tag along, I could have filled another book with all the excuses I was given. Clearly all my friends were wimps who didn't fancy it if it wasn't somewhere warm, with comfy hotels and good food, and riot police who mostly abstained from beating you up first and, if still possible, then asking the questions. The first ten or so get-outs I was given for ducking out of the Poland trip were as follows: hospital appointment, business meeting, niece's christening, can't afford it, got to take the goldfish to the vet, Friday Night is Supermarket Night, lost my passport, granny's birthday/funeral, don't want to miss Big Brother, and 'just been there on holiday'.

YOU COME WITH ME - I GET TICKETS

That last one was unlikely, as we happened to be talking about Belarus (Poland's opponents last Saturday in Lodz) at the time, but I can take a hint and pretended not to have smelt this very evident rat. One person at least was honest, leaving me in no doubt that he would sooner nail a very painful part of his anatomy to a brick than stand on a terrace in, where did you say it was again? Um, well it's in Lodz actually, which is sort of a large, grimy and not terribly nice industrial city, you're sure to like it there, and the weather in the middle of October is certain to be pleasant. Hello?

This funny foreigners, dodgy water, can't-get-a-McDonald's attitude that you still find in Britain can be depressing sometimes. It reminds me of the insularity that led to the post-Keegan, got-to-have-an-English-manager-for-the-England-team campaign. We English invented the game and so, by definition and in perpetuity, only we know what's best. But in November 2000, after that autumn's qualifying fixtures, Keegan's resignation, the home defeat to Germany and Ray Parlour's - yes, Ray Parlour's - scuffed effort that clearly didn't cross the Finnish line, England shared with Malta, Azerbaijan, Moldova, San Marino, Latvia and Liechtenstein the distinction of having scored zero goals in the qualifying tournament to date, while high-flying Andorra had scored three times, Estonia four and Switzerland seven. Albania, who had been walloped at a canter by Finland, were nevertheless two points ahead of England. But so many of us in the land where football was born like to stay in the familiar old rut of a game of two halves, it was a midfield battle out there today but the boys done great and now for Hartlepool next week. Thankfully, as we now know, there were those prepared to look a bit further afield.

I brought my beer back out onto the terrace of the Pele, because outside there was still room to breathe and the air smelt less strongly of sheep. Some of the twenty or so Ukrainians were out here as well, sinking their first beers of the night and complaining about how expensive the beer was compared to Copenhagen last week. And then there was Paris last year of course, pity Zidane didn't play that night. I began to wonder how come I was understanding this. They were speaking English to each other, that's how come I was understanding this. Seeing as it was unlikely to be for my benefit that they were doing so, I asked one of them how come he spoke the language so fluently. I decided to pick on him because the giant evil-smelling woolly Cossack-style sheepskin hat he had on was the closest object to my face.

'Because I come from Milwaukee,' he said, resisting any temptation he might have felt to chin me for not recognising what he probably thought was a standard US accent. 'There's over twenty of us here, but only two of us have come from Ukraine for this game.'

'That's right mate,' said a big lad also wearing a woolly hat which had the size, if not the elegance, of a domestic wheelie bin. I took a step back, bumping into assorted velvet-hatted Vikings as I did so. Ukraine's economy wasn't the strongest, but if their sheep were this big before being turned into kebabs, rugs and headgear, the country's agricultural and clothing sectors should be cleaning up against all-comers. He was carrying a huge drum which pointed outwards from his not inconsiderable stomach. Whack! went the drum. 'I'm from Stockport. Half of us here are from the US and the rest are mainly from the UK. We all get together for Ukraine games abroad. We don't go to all the matches, so we missed the game against Armenia the other day. But we won that!' Boom! Yes: 3-2 in Yerevan, Shevchenko getting a couple. 'We were in Denmark last week and we'll have a few days in Sweden before we go home.'

'So,' I asked, 'are you Ukrainian or not?'

'Second generation. Our parents all spoke Ukrainian and so do we. We're a bit scattered across the world, and we speak English in everyday life, in our jobs and so on, but this is a good way for us to meet up and be properly Ukrainian for a bit. Amongst ourselves, we speak Ukrainian.' Except when reminiscing about trips to Paris or complaining about the price of beer, obviously. He looked round and shouted something, in Ukrainian for a change. It sounded like an order.

'Oh no,' my new friend from Milwaukee groaned in response. 'Now we dance.' Evidently this was part of the Ukrainian build-up to every game. It was the drummer's job to get the lads in line for a spot of traditional woolly-hatted arms-and-legs-crossed leaping about. Crash! Wallop! Amazed Norwegians stood and watched as a dozen or more Ukrainian fans, many of whom, it has to be said, were not displaying the very greatest enthusiasm for all this, got down to the task of performing what looked like the Red Army Circus On Tour crossed with One Man And His Dog. In fact several of them were looking sheepish in more ways than one, including Mr Reluctant of Milwaukee. After all, on most days, this was a standard narrow suburban walkway lined with shoe shops, travel agents and jewellers, probably not what the original nomadic herdsmen had had in mind as a backdrop when they choreographed this stuff. Homeward-bound commuters applauded self-consciously.

By now even the terrace of the bar was getting full, and overzealous stewardy jobsworth types were hauling back anyone who stepped a fraction of an inch onto the pavement while still carrying a drink. Unenthusiastic at the prospect of watching more dancing outside, I moved back in and met up with two very un-Ukrainian looking lads called Hakan and Per Ivar. There was no reason why they should have started talking to me but when several dozen large Norwegian football supporters in a confined space decide they all want another beer at the same time to escape the mandatory Cossack dancing show, the resulting shove can push people together. Per Ivar lost no time telling me he was a trainee electrician, and a Liverpool fan. He kept singing bits of Britney Spears songs, as he'd paid what sounded like vastly over the odds for a ticket on the forthcoming Scandinavian leg of the Britney World Tour. He didn't seem to mind the ribbing he was taking from his mates about this and about how he was going to be the oldest person at the show. He looked about 24, zimmer-frame age by Britney standards.

Hakan meanwhile described himself as a 'rich student' and a Tottenham fan who'd also been an electrician once, or else he was training to become one. He'd done his knee in, playing handball, which appeared to be a good part of the reason he was now a student again. As for being a Spurs fan, to be honest it was a relief to find someone in Scandinavia who didn't support either Liverpool or Man U. Tottenham players were set to feature heavily in tonight's game, with a newly-signed and still confident Sergei Rebrov on the Ukrainian side, and Steffen Iversen and Oyvind Leonhardsen for the Norwegians. 'I hope Norway win 3-2,' said Hakan, 'three goals from Iversen and then two from Rebrov just before the end.' Club can appear to come before country in Norway as well.

Unlike in Finland, the concept of a round of drinks seems to have made some headway in Norway. Hakan was buying first. He looked at his new not-quite-pint, on the top of which sat at least an inch and a half of snowy froth, and then looked at me. 'This beer is like Arsenal,' he said. 'Too much scum.' I resisted the temptation to point out that it was Spurs who played in white. Behind him a noxious off-white sheepskin hat was deep in conversation with a sanitised velvety blue and red Viking hat. By now, somewhere from deep inside the bar, Stockport's finest had finished conducting his al fresco floor show. He was testing out his drum every few seconds, and generally being Ukrainian in a way I thought he probably wouldn't get away with on a Thursday night when it was time to do the Sainsbury's run. I asked Hakan and Per Ivar what Norwegians did after international football matches.

'After the game? Depends if we win. If we win, we'll be back here. If we lose, straight home.'

We drank up our beers and went off to find our seats. Round the back of the stadium a blue and red-clad brass band was tuning up along with a bunch of people calling themselves the 'Football Kor' - the first choir I'd ever seen at a football match. But then, this was Norway. Sheets of music were being eagerly handed out and folded to fit. Meanwhile local or national TV were doing pre-match interviews next to the turnstiles with people I couldn't recognise but who the locals clearly did. I'd left it pretty late to find my seat. The anthems were already over and the Ukrainian players' names were being cheerfully booed by the crowd when I got to my place, climbing over an elderly man who had evidently ended up with the spare ticket I'd originally bought but sold to a tout. I couldn't bring myself to ask how much he'd paid for it: probably a lot more than I got for it.

YOU COME WITH ME - I GET TICKETS

This was the fourth game I'd seen and the first in a full, modern stadium under lights. Any sport played under lights has an extra special atmosphere to it, and despite the rain which began to fall now and which continued for the rest of the evening, and despite Norway's unfair reputation for cool northern European reserve, there was a cracking atmosphere. The place was packed, the lights were dazzling, the big replay screens were going, and the noise was intense. My seat was two rows back from the Ukrainian goal, close enough to see who sponsored the 'keeper's boots and the whites of his eyes when he was tearing strips off his defenders. 'Dream Football, Scream Football, Drink Coca Cola' yelled banners all around the top tier of the stadium. As in Finland, the schoolkids - and there seemed to be plenty of school parties - nearly all had their faces painted in the national colours. The PA man had two more things up his sleeve before we could get under way. One was a replay of the commentary from the moment of Norway's epoch-making (for them anyway) 1981 win over England, you know the one: 'Lord Nelson, Winston Churchill, Lady Diana, Maggie Thatcher, can you hear me, your boys took a hell of a beating,' yes, that one. I was able to cheer myself up by listening to the announcer's final offering, the Norway squad's smash hit Euro 2000 number, played before every game to whip up the crowd - the frankly awe-inspiring 'We Are Farmers From The North'. Take it from me - a rival to the All Blacks' haka it is not.

The game was fairly even to begin with, Norway having maybe the better of the chances. As the game went on, Norway's chances got better and the misses more blatant. Their strikers had been having a terrible time of it for several games now, just unable to bury the chances created. It was still 0-0 at the halftime break. A bloke in a standard issue Viking bobble hat was using the facilities in the gents with one hand while carrying on a mobile phone call with the other, probably telling his wife how much longer he was going to be. Then it was time for something to eat - and tonight's hot dog was the best I'd yet had, knocking spots off last Saturday's gristle-filled Polish one.

Four minutes into the second half, Shevchenko tucked away a pass from Vorobei for his fourth goal in Ukraine's three qualifying games so far, and that was it. Solskjaer should have levelled it a few minutes from the end but whacked it over the bar instead. Erik Mykland had Norway's last chance, but shot wide. Throughout the second half the atmosphere dampened, literally and figuratively, with every minute that went by. Even the brass band and the Football Kor up in the top tier were packing away their tubas by the time 75 minutes were up, to the relief of just about everyone. The rain may have prevented either side from playing really creatively, but with all those chances Norway should never have lost. 25,000 went home despondent.

Despite threatening to go home Hakan and Per Ivar were back in the Pele Bar to drown their sorrows. They waved me over and I bought them another fizzy plastic pint to cheer them up. Solskjaer had had a nightmare game and wasn't worth his reputed £30,000 a week, they said. No. 18 shirt Thorstein Helstad should have come on before the 76th minute. That was it for Norway's chances of reaching Korea/Japan 2002 now. Per Ivar was staying cheerful, on the surface at least. 'Spurs lost this game' he gleefully told his friend, meaning that the side containing the greater number of Spurs players (Norway, by 2 to 1) had lost. After this he went over to congratulate some of the Ukrainian fans who, perhaps less surprisingly, had also reappeared in the bar. A second compulsory dancing session was instigated. Per Ivar swallowed his pride and strutted his stuff with a floppy sheepskin hat on his head. I told him he should hang on to it, as he would look the part in one of those at the Britney Spears gig in a few days' time.

'Those hats are hot!' he replied, meaning, I hoped, in terms of temperature rather than style or desirability. We started to talk about the consistent popularity of English football in Scandinavia. Liverpool played in Norway each pre-season, according to Per Ivar, and that was a big reason why the club was so well supported there. As everywhere else, opinions about Manchester United were sharply divided. For all his backing of the Norwegian players in the Spurs team, Hakan thought there were too many non-English players in the Premiership and that England needed to look no further than that to explain their recent poor international results. He clearly knew his English football, having lived in Leeds for twelve months and London for six. 'Gazza's goal in Euro '96 was the best by an Englishman at Wembley,' he said.

'Yes,' I agreed. 'That's the best goal I ever saw there as well.'

'No,' said Hakan. 'I only mean the best English goal. The best Wembley goal ever was Kjetil Rekdal's for Norway against you in 1994.' Thanks, pal. Another beer?

Three or four of Hakan and Per Ivar's friends, all of them apparently future or ex-electricians, had arrived in the bar as well by now. One of them looked alarmingly like a pre-pony-tailed David Seaman but, more usefully, he drove a beat-up old VW Golf which he had just casually parked about 5 yards away, right outside a main entrance to the stadium. They decided to carry on in a bar in central Oslo and invited me along with them, so after a major detour through the suburbs to collect or drop off enough Norwegian apprentice electricians to fit out a whole estate, we ended up at an 'Internet bar'. Apparently, exciting footage from this place was broadcast live on the Internet for half an hour every day and, this being Norway, viewers could vote to expel their least-liked bar-staff or regulars, like that barman, the one in the green hat. At least there wasn't a choir here.

Towards midnight, as the place was emptying (this was a Wednesday in October in Oslo), I said goodbye and came back to my hotel, which Hakan and Per Ivar took great delight in informing me was in the red light district. I wondered how they knew that, but perhaps they'd done the lighting for the area as part of their training. By way of fond farewell, I told Hakan and Per Ivar that when they came to England I'd buy them beer that was twice as good as the stuff they'd bought me, at half the price and served in a proper glass. But seeing as I was someone they'd never met, both Hakan and Per Ivar had been far more welcoming towards me than I had any right to expect from anyone.

Next morning, I read what *Aftenposten*, Oslo's main quality paper, had to say about yesterday's game. Here's the headlines I could make out: 'On the Way Out of the World Cup', 'Norway Can't Score Any More', and 'More Trouble For Norway' - because Belarus had beaten Armenia to go second in the group behind Poland, who got a point from a draw with Wales. Despite two wins from three games, Ukraine were only in third place. Copious colour pictures showed hunched Norwegian players trudging off, or dejected coach Nils Johan Semb, surrounded by photographers and making the legendarily ashen-faced Ron Knee look like Ron Atkinson after his summer break. Semb offered his resignation next day, and got the dreaded 'vote of confidence' treatment from the Norwegian Football Association, according to whom 'the recent weak results' did not affect the Association's long-term plans. A year later, despite further poor results, he was still in charge. For now, Norwegian football came away from the Ukraine fixture in sombre mood.

6.

Aye, They'll Get a Few, Right Enough

Belgium - San Marino, Roi Baudouin Stadium, Brussels, Wednesday 28 February 2001

IT FELT LIKE A BAD MISTAKE. On the day of England's 3-0 win against Spain in a friendly, Sven-Goran Eriksson's first game in charge, I could have been in the winter sun in Madeira watching the Portugal game. Instead I had somehow ended up in Brussels to watch the locals take on mighty San Marino.

Although this was a date set aside for international football, the only two 'competitive' matches being played tonight were Belgium's game in qualifying group 6, and Portugal's against Andorra in whatever group they were in. The other international matches being played were all friendlies, and I'd decided from the outset only to watch competitive matches. In reality of course, neither of tonight's World Cup qualifiers would actually be in any way competitive, as neither San Marino nor Andorra stood the slightest chance of getting a result (apart from a total shoeing, that is, but defeat is not a 'result'). I'd already seen Portugal play, so it had to be Belgium.

For the geographically challenged, Madeira is an island in the Atlantic a couple of hours south-west of Portugal by air, and is famous for warm and sunny weather in early spring. Whereas Brussels in February is, well, Brussels in February. This did not feel like perfect planning on my part.

AYE, THEY'LL GET A FEW, RIGHT ENOUGH

In fact the weather, in the words of the Carling Black Label ad, had turned out nice again. I rang up from the airport to reserve a room and sat in the sun on the train into the city. But I still needed to persuade myself again that I hadn't really wanted to go to sun-drenched, sub-tropical Madeira at all. After all, why travel all that way when there was a game in Belgium? The temperature, which could have been as high as seventy degrees, would probably be too much of a shock after an English winter. Andorra were spectacularly useless, and I'd seen the Portuguese wallop Estonia only a few months ago. Much better to go to this game, in Scotland's group, and see how Belgium were shaping up for their big clash with Craig Brown's team in Glasgow on March 24.

Also, for me coming from England, history had cast a shadow as well. Tonight's game was in the King Baudouin stadium, scene of the opening fixture of Euro 2000, a stadium previously, and more notoriously, known as Heysel. After the tragic events of May 1985 it was easy to see why the Belgian authorities had wanted to change the name of the stadium when it was rebuilt, but the metro station where you leave the train on your way to the ground is still Heysel.

If Andorra stood no chance against Portugal then neither, in all fairness, did San Marino against Belgium, although there was of course that superb goal they scored against England in 1993, straight from the kick-off when their one and only striker ran on to an underhit back pass from an England defender to take an extremely early lead. Boringly for all supporters of the underdog, England then came back to win 7-1. Oh well. Maybe tonight they'd do something just as wacky.

My hotel was on Stalingrad Avenue. I had to remind myself that this was Brussels, not Ceaucescu's Bucharest, and that the place would be perfectly pleasant. It was, apart from the dangling wires in the reception area lift, which was one of those French, alleged 'four persons' efforts, one of those where you had to really like the other three you were in it with or hope at least that they'd showered that morning.

My room was very dark indeed, because it didn't have a window. It was also not very large; if anything, it made the lift appear spacious. Close investigation revealed a tiny curtain at knee height in one wall, which turned out to conceal a window about eighteen inches square, with an attractive view of a concrete stairwell designed by the kind of brain that gave us high-rise housing estates. It could have been a fire escape, but anyone passing would have had a distinctly close-up view into the room. I closed the curtain again and turned on a few more lights. The room certainly made up in artificial light what it lacked in the real thing.

It was late afternoon. The TV was showing Prime Minister's Questions on the BBC and rip-offs of Countdown in six European languages on all the other channels. I turned it off and opened the newspaper I'd bought from the newsagent's over the road from the hotel in order to see how things were shaping up for tonight's game.

The first thing that surprised me was that 40,000 tickets had been sold (or as the paper said, 'distributed', which may have been a euphemism for 'handed out free to schoolkids') and that the last 5,000 would be on sale on the day of the game - today. I had thought it unlikely that San Marino would be much of a must-see attraction, even for Belgians, and so I'd planned to just mosey along a little while before kick-off and pay at the gate. Maybe it wouldn't be so easy. The Belgian press (or this bit of it anyway) obviously wasn't familiar with the phrase 'potential banana skin'. This game was just a gimme for three points, as far as they were concerned. Two or three of the Belgian side looked set to make their debuts tonight. 'They couldn't dream of a more comfortable start in international football than tonight', purred *La Derniere Heure*. A big picture showed an electronic scoreboard with the 6-0 scoreline by which Belgium had 'easily' won the last meeting between the sides in 1997. 'Even Better This Time?' was the front page headline underneath it. 'Belgium are expected to do even better tonight, or at least as well, with an inexperienced team', went the report. Maybe, just maybe, all this would backfire. After all, Scotland had only won 2-0 last October and Latvia had only scored once when they met San Marino in November. I was looking forward to a famous upset. I didn't get one.

AYE, THEY'LL GET A FEW, RIGHT ENOUGH

After walking the wrong way, most of the way round the stadium complex, I found the offices where tickets were on sale. There were thousands still available, and mine was in the front row of a new block they were starting to sell the tickets for. Then I bought a tasteful 'Red Devils' T-shirt and went off to look for something to eat. The Red Devils (or 'Les Diables Rouges' or 'de Rode Duivels', depending which bit of Belgium you're from) is the nickname of the Belgian team, who were going into this game three points behind group leaders Scotland but with this game in hand. Provided they won, they would go to Glasgow as group leader (or 'en Leader' as Belgian French authentically has it) - if only on goal difference. Their goal difference was already one better then the Scots', despite having played a game less, and everyone knew the importance of whacking quite a few past the San Marinese, as I think they're called. A healthy goal difference would be as good as an extra point when the group games were over.

I spotted a likely-looking Turkish-run kebab joint on the other side of the superbly named Avenue Houba de Strooper, the main road which runs along one side of the stadium. Belgians jaywalk more fearlessly than most law-abiding West Europeans, but I stood waiting for the lights to change, and three people joined me and waited too. They were Scots. With Belgium due in Glasgow the following month, maybe they'd come to take an early look at their next opposition. But they weren't heading for the same kebab place so I thought no more of them, and bought a non-specific 'meat kebab', which I survived. Now it was time for a beer.

Back up near the stadium entrance was 'Le Corner', presumably 'le Leader' among bars near the ground. Inflatable rubber tridents and other authentic Red Devils merchandise bristled around the counter. Beer was of a pre-determined type served in hooligan-proof plastic cups, but it was good, as the Belgians do know a thing or two about beer, even if it is fizzy. Unlike in Oslo, there were no visiting fans in sheepskin hats, or whatever the San Marino national costume is, in this bar, so I drank up and headed on up the road.

Sitting near the window of the hotel next door to Le Corner was Scotland manager Craig Brown, with three apparatchiks in suits who I now recognised as the people I'd crossed the road with near the kebab bar. It didn't need what a friend of mine calls rocket surgery to work out why they were here.

Craig Brown, being articulate and in possession of a dry sense of humour, is - or was - of a different mould to most managers. I walked in and sat down at the next table, thinking I might overhear the Scottish game-plan for their March 24 meeting with the Belgians or something. The four of them, ties on but jackets off, looked like any group of businessmen meeting over drinks before dinner. I finished the coffee I'd ordered and on my way out, having failed to overhear many secrets, I told them that I was the only other spectator at tonight's game who'd be rooting for San Marino. Coming from an Englishman, they took that pretty well. I asked Craig Brown how many he thought Belgium would win by. 'Aye, they'll get a few, right enough,' he said, 'unfortunately.' As Belgium were to score ten that night, he was of course correct, but not in a way he would have wanted, you felt.

Nearly kick-off time. Stadium security asked if I had anything dangerous on me, but I didn't even have a blow-up red, yellow and black plastic trident. My block of seats was empty, so clearly either no one else had bought a ticket after me or the locals were treating this game Finnish-style by staying away right up until the start - 20 minutes to go and the place was only a third full. In fact the Belgians had worked out a refinement of the Finnish technique. Here the fans missed so much of the first half it was nearer to half time than kick-off time when they finally sauntered in. Perhaps this was their way of appearing cool, detached and confident - to them, arriving at the game late must mean they knew their team would already be in the lead, just as fans leaving early in Britain know their team has lost.

The scoreboard gave everyone an English language 'Heartly Welcome' to the stadium, and I began to notice how much of the official language on things was in English. The names of the countries on the scoreboard were in English, and across the back of the official jackets and kit tops it said 'Belgium'. The country is almost evenly divided between Flemish and French speakers, each group being fiercely protective of its language. Many a Belgian national team has lacked for support in one half of the country owing to a perceived bias in selection - too many Flemish speakers, or an entirely French-speaking defence, that kind of thing. Maybe having everything in neither national language but in English instead was a compromise designed to save a lot of time and argument. If you can't have it your way, at least stop the other lot from having it their way; or if you can't beat them, whatever you do, don't join them.

Belgium scored after 10 minutes. From the word go they gave every indication that it was only a matter of time, so the crowd never got restless. German-based Emile Mpenza, definitely a crowd favourite after his eye-catching performances in Euro 2000, got a second two minutes later, and even though Belgium only added one more in the last half hour of the first half, the celebrations could begin. The Red Devils' territorial domination was so complete that de Vlieger in the Belgian goal was up near the centre circle at times, trying to keep himself both warm and involved. Mexican waves rippled around the stadium, with the standard booing of the corporate hospitality set in the lower tier of the main stand for their failure to join in. The waves died down for a minute while everyone celebrated the third goal, and then round they went again. The singing started in earnest as well. Before long, the fans had launched into a heavily accented version of the marvellous, tradition-steeped Low Countries number, 'We love you Belgium, we do (repeat twice), oh Belgium, we love you'.

As it was a cold night, de Vlieger came out after half time with an armchair and slippers, and settled down with a newspaper and colour supplement (a goalie mag, perhaps) in front of a fire he proceeded to build out of his own redundant goalposts. All right, I might have made that up. But he could just as well have done. San Marino had held on grimly throughout the middle of the game, but were swept away in the last half hour, letting in goals after 50, 60, 64, 72, 76, 84 and 88 minutes. Over on the far side of the ground, the first conga started at 6-0. Apart from English fans on TV, Belgians were the only ones I saw anywhere do a conga. Bob Peeters, a front player with the build of a rugby no.8, came on with under half an hour to go, and scored a hat-trick. 'We Want Ten!' went the cry after Peeters had tucked away his second to increase the home side's lead to 9-0. With six minutes left on the clock and with a nine-goal lead, this was beginning to look comfortable for Belgium. Four minutes later Peeters granted the crowd their wish, by taking Belgium into double figures for the biggest win in their history - a 9-0 against Zambia some years earlier had been Belgium's previous best. San Marino only slightly took off the gloss by scoring from a powerful free kick with one minute to go, thereby not only scoring their first goal in the 2002 World Cup campaign at an earlier calendar date than England, but also turning this into merely their second worst thrashing, avoiding a repeat of their 10-0 fiasco against Norway back in 1992. You felt that if de Vlieger had had more to do in the first 89 minutes of the game, he'd have kept out that free kick, but the poor guy must have been either frozen or fast asleep.

All around me, normally sober-minded Belgians were going nuts about all this. The scoreboard ran out of space to list the scorers' names after eight goals, so the last two Red Devils net bulgers went unrecorded. In fact only four scorers' names fitted onto the main screen at any one time, so the operators alternated two screens, in a Ceefax-style 'Page 2 of 2' sort of trick to display the scorers of goals five to eight. Peeters' last two goals were just taken as read. Almost as much as the size of the win, and the practically unassailable goal difference Belgium had now racked up, the crowd appreciated the style of the goals. As far as I can remember none of them was the result of an untidy goalmouth scramble or a lucky deflection. Several, including Peeters' goals in particular, were powerful shots from range, and one was the most bullet-like header I've ever seen. OK, so it was only San Marino, but this was truly some win. Often the San Marino players were left on the ground by the force of perfectly fair tackles.

This was Belgium, so the crowd soon calmed down and melted away, pretty happy with life but not about to paint the town anything like Red. I thought better of trying to find Craig Brown again and asking him what he thought about this result, partly because the smack in the mouth the question would have deserved might have offended me, but more because the answer was obvious. It made defeating the Belgians in March all the more important, as the Scots were unlikely to recover the ground in the goal difference column even with their own home game against San Marino - in fact all their home games - still to come.

Back at the hotel, the Portugal-Andorra game was still going on, live on a Portuguese channel somehow available in Brussels. I watched the last 20 minutes, and quickly established that the rain there was torrential, that everyone was waiting for it to end so as to go home and get dry, that Portugal had had it wrapped up since a Figo goal in the second minute, and that I'd had better weather right here in Brussels.

Next day's Belgian papers made hay over their team's record-breaking win. '10-1: Un Score Historique!', opined *La Derniere Heure*. For *La Gazette des Sports* the result was also, funnily enough, 'historique.' Mpenza, Vanderhaeghe and the rest were in colour on the front pages, and the Scots were left quaking in their boots.

7.

I Finish Early,
Today Is Football

Romania - Italy, Ghencea Stadium, Bucharest, Saturday 24 March 2001

BY BEING MARGINALLY the more competitive, on paper at least, of the two games played on the February date for international matches, Belgium's 10-1 demolition of San Marino had been a bit of an extra. But, with a result like that, it wasn't so much end-to-end stuff as back-up-the-same-end-yet-again stuff. The eleven goals had certainly made it fun to watch, but for next time I wanted something more competitive.

The qualifying campaign only really resumed in earnest in March, so I had plenty of time over the winter to think about where to go for the back-to-back 24 and 28 March fixtures. As I'd been mostly to northern Europe so far, it was high time to go south - as well as to look for matches that would be more of a contest. The fixture list offered ample choice - on March 24 Austria were in Sarajevo to take on Bosnia, in a repeat of their big August 1914 clash (and look at the mess that got everybody into). Then after that, to get to England's game in Albania, it would be a quick hop down the coast to Tirana.

I spent a bit of time looking into this. It quickly became obvious that, although Bosnia haven't really cut the mustard yet at international level, football is massive in the country. Not that you'd know it from the attention it gets in the British sports media, however, where Bosnian football only gets a mention when teams like Zeljeznicar have the effrontery to try to qualify for the Champions' League at the expense of Newcastle, a fourth English Premiership team. And as for the game in Tirana, it seemed a fair bet that very few English fans would pick that one out, which was why it attracted me.

The alternative was Bucharest, for Italy's visit on Saturday March 24, followed by Athens for Greece against Germany the following Wednesday. Watching both Italy and Germany take on tough away fixtures within four days was an attractive prospect, and I decided to go for it. Romania, as Euro 2000 veteran Phil Neville would doubtless confirm, were no slouches themselves, and the Greeks knew a thing or two about getting behind their team - and sometimes at them instead. Also, I'd already seen Albania play, and they hadn't done much to tempt me back for more.

Then a friend of mine, who travels on business to Tirana from time to time, said she could get tickets for the Albania-England game, in person from the Permanent Secretary in the Albanian Ministry of Finance. I'd be rubbing shoulders with all the chiefs from the World Bank and other economic assistance outfits with a presence in the country. She also said she had dozens of football-mad contacts in Bosnia who she could put me in touch with. As a place to go, she said, Sarajevo was now fine, and as it appeared to be about the only place you could get to Tirana from, it would be on my route anyway. For social life, she said, Sarajevo was just like Prague, with an even higher density of bars, cafes and restaurants. Oh, and then there were the Bosnian Serb bullet holes in every building, and countless unexploded landmines in every patch of ground that wasn't tarmac. As for the airport, it was so littered with burnt-out, unserviceable vehicles and aircraft that it made the Wacky Races starting grid look like a BMW showroom. Was I sure I didn't want to go to Sarajevo?

I nearly did change my mind, but I thought the Albanian Minister of Finance might take offence if I sat in his seat by mistake. And anyway, by now I'd got my ticket for Bucharest.

Unlike some places, Romania was not a country where I fancied trying to get a ticket at the last minute. A World Cup qualifier against Italy would undoubtedly pull in a capacity crowd, so I tried to find a friendly local who might be able to help. A lad called Sorin told me that the tickets would be sold, to personal callers only, at the three main club stadiums in Bucharest - Steaua, Rapid, and Dinamo. Unfortunately, he said, as he lived in Suceava, a town about 300 miles from Bucharest, he couldn't help me any further. Tickets would go on sale on 19 March, he said, five days before the game, and unless you happened to be in Bucharest that day or soon after, you had no chance.

One or two other helpful fans had told me what the ticket prices were likely to be. Thirty US dollars (that's the kind of economy Romania has) would get you the best seat in the house and probably some corporate prawn sandwiches into the bargain. Twenty dollar seats were perfectly good as well, while ten dollars got you a place behind the goalkeeper. However, these were the black market prices, for which I guessed you had to show up behind a shed in the street next to the ground. Officially, just over ten dollars was the top price - still big money in a country where the average monthly wage works out at around $120. Another possibility was a travel/ticket agency in Bucharest that Sorin believed would handle tickets for the game, but I felt I wanted a bit more personal control than that seemed to offer.

All in all it seemed likely that by the time I got there on the Friday afternoon, the day before the game, all the tickets would have gone. Being picked up by the Romanian police for black market ticket dealings was not part of my plans. Neither was failing to get in and having to watch the game on TV somewhere. I had no idea whether the Romanian boys in blue would distinguish between buyer and seller in an unofficial ticketing transaction, although having made all the other arrangements for this trip I might have no option but to try and get a ticket this way. Then another of my speculative e-mail contacts, Romeo (pronounced as in Alfa, rather than Beckham junior), got in touch.

He could probably help me, he said, but he wasn't sure if he would be going to the game himself. To help him make up his mind, I offered to pay for his ticket as well, if he was just able to get his hands on a couple. But he still didn't, or couldn't, commit himself. There were a few problems. He lived in Ploiesti, an oil-producing town only about an hour by car from Bucharest, but his car was off the road. It was still early March, and with the whole country under a blanket of snow, driving was not an option for him. Also, the kick-off was not until 9.30pm local time, which may or may not have been to do with the requirements of Italian TV. After all, excessive heat and humidity were unlikely to be factors in Romania in March. Whatever the reason, it meant that the game would finish at 11.15pm at the earliest, and with the crowds and Romanian roads, that meant a 2am return home for him, presumably past his bedtime.

My hopes of both seeing this game and avoiding the back of a Romanian police van were beginning to depend more and more on me persuading Romeo that a great game was in prospect, and that what he really wanted to do was dig his car out of the snowdrift where it had apparently spent most of the winter, get it fixed, and then drive the thing to Bucharest and buy a couple of tickets. Time was running out for me to make other (legal) efforts to get a ticket if he turned out to be unable or unwilling to do this - and let's face it, it was a big ask. Was someone from England really going to come to see Romania play Italy? His initial outlay could be up to 20 dollars. Would he spend that amount of money on the tickets and take the chance that I wasn't just a hoaxer or a timewaster, but someone who would actually show up?

It began to look as if he would. About a week before the game, he told me he'd had his car sorted and would head for Bucharest on Monday, the day the tickets went on sale. Fantastic. But on Tuesday it all went wrong. He scanned over a newspaper feature to me, which showed hundreds of patient Romanian fans queuing to get a ticket. The article explained that these fans had queued for four hours outside Steaua Bucharest's Ghencea stadium, where the game was to be played. In those four hours, 3,200 tickets had been sold and that looked to be about it. It looked like I'd drawn a blank. But I had my air ticket and so I was committed. I'll go anyway, I thought, and what happens, happens. I'd get in somehow, probably thanks to the almighty dollar.

Looked at one way, ticket touting is the pure market, prices determined by supply and demand. Personally I wouldn't sell a ticket above face value, but I've bought them at a mark-up before now because they were worth it to me at the time. It would be dark in Bucharest well before kick-off and not even the Romanian police could be everywhere. Quite likely, touting was so standard that they'd turn a blind eye. I'd probably be OK if I was careful and chose my moment.

By Thursday evening I had a wad of dollars and I was ready to go, when Romeo got back in touch to say he'd gone to Bucharest earlier that day - he hadn't gone on Monday after all, having heard about the queues. But he'd waited in line that Thursday for five minutes at one of the stadiums selling tickets, bought two, and driven home. Simple, really. I rang him up, told him what a great job he'd done, and gave him directions to the hotel I'd be in so we could meet for a drink before the game. Warning me about 'prostituates' in my hotel, he wished me a good trip.

Carrying a Romanian sports newspaper to make myself look more like a local, and a glossy map which made me look a lot less like one, I walked out of the terminal building at Bucharest airport to get the bus into town. Unfortunately, I couldn't immediately see the bus stop, and that fractional hesitation was all it took for the airport taxi spivs to smell blood. Within ten seconds I'd picked up four of them.

'Hello. Where you from? You want taxi into city? Ten dollars, is good for you, official twenty.'

'No thanks, I'm going by bus. Can you tell me where the stop is, please?'

'Bus very bad. Very slow. I have good car. You come.'

'That's OK, I'm in no rush. Where did you say the stop was?'

'No, you come with me. Where your hotel? Ten dollars, is fair price, official is twenty.'

'Five dollars,' I said, knowing that locals would pay three or four at the most. I spotted the bus stop and set off, with the spiv pack in pursuit, only to find it was the wrong bus stop. I gave up, settled for seven dollars, and climbed aboard one of Romania's finest private transport options.

I FINISH EARLY, TODAY IS FOOTBALL

'I finish early today, today is football,' said my driver. I guessed he meant the Romania-Italy Under-21 game, due to be played tonight. Seven dollars was probably a whole day's takings, so he could afford to knock off early.

'I'm here for the football as well, the World Cup game tomorrow night,' I said.

'You come for this game? You are Italian?'

It took a minute or two to persuade him that I didn't just speak English, I actually was English. 'Are you going to the game tomorrow? Have you got a ticket?' I asked him. According to Romeo, the game was now sold out.

'You want ticket for Romania-Italia? It will cost fifty dollars.'

Would it now. 'No, my friend's got me one. I was asking if you were going.'

He shrugged. 'I hope so. Maybe I will have to work. Romania have no chance. The team change so much.'

'Is Hagi playing?'

'Hagi - finish. Popescu - finish. Petrescu and Moldovan - finish.'

'What happened with Petrescu then - did he say he was retiring from international football, or did the Romanian manager decide not to pick him any more? You know, did he jump or was he pushed?'

'Yes.'

Oh well. According to Romeo, there'd been some story about Petrescu not turning up to model the new Romanian kit, and there had been something of an argument.

We talked a bit about tonight's Under-21 game. I'd got up at three that morning for the flight east, but if I wasn't too wiped out I'd thought of going myself. He showed me where it was being played, and kindly offered to let me pay him further dollars to drive me there from my hotel, which we'd now reached. Thanks all the same, I said, but I'd make my own way, if I went at all. That's why I'd bought the glossy map.

'How long you stay in Romania?'

'I'm leaving on Sunday, by train to Bulgaria.'

'You want taxi for Sunday, to railway station?'

YOU COME WITH ME - I GET TICKETS

Neither of the two receptionists could find any trace of my reservation. The hotel was a converted factory, out in the northern suburbs, in a part of the city the receptionist had described over the phone as 'green'. This was accurate, provided you focused only on the pondweed in the nearby boating lake. Otherwise, describing anywhere in Bucharest as 'green' was stretching a point, certainly in March. The urban landscape makes the set of the Mad Max movies look about as post-nuclear as Miss Marple. Unfinished concrete buildings loom everywhere, several storeys high but often lacking a complete set of external walls; there are merely concrete pillars, floors with steel cables poking out, and dark holes for the windows, and it's a pretty brutal sight all in all. At fifth or sixth storey level in the city centre, the facades of once imposing old buildings are pockmarked with bullet holes from the big Christmas 1989 shootout with the former dictator Ceaucescu's Securitate.

Another endearing feature is the way that every patch of waste ground and many pavements are home to stray dogs. There were several roaming loose in the grounds of the hotel, and well over a million in the city overall. Romeo, when I met him later, explained that no one really knew what to do about them. Some people favoured bringing in the Army to do a cull, but others objected to that, possibly thinking that in a fragile democracy like Romania's, allowing the Army loose on the streets with a licence to take potshots whenever they felt like it might have one or two unintended consequences. These animals were mostly of little threat, but you could never be certain, and I was bitten on the ankle within three hours of arriving. Rabies is rare, and my shoe took the brunt of it, but I had a good long look to see if the skin had been punctured.

'How did you make your reservation?' asked one receptionist.

'By e-mail,' I said.

'Ah,' said the two of them together, looking at each other. 'The manager is out of the country, and all reservations come through on his account, which we cannot access while he is away. But fortunately we have many rooms available.' With administration procedures like that, it was no wonder they had many rooms available. The place was practically empty. There weren't even any prostituates. Maybe they'd all gone to a hotel that actually had some guests.

After settling in I left the hotel to get my bearings, which amounted to seeing where the metro station was, collecting the dog bite on the way back, and establishing that the nearest convivial bar was probably in Hungary. The Under-21 game was live on national TV, so I got a meal in the hotel, watched some of the game, checked my ankle again and fell asleep.

I had time the next morning to see the sights, such as they were. But first I needed to buy a train ticket and, I hoped, a sleeper reservation for the trip to Sofia on Sunday night, so I went to the combined national train/airline ticket agency in the city centre. There were only three other customers when I arrived, and a remarkable eight staff on duty.

'Sofia, one-way tomorrow night, with a sleeper,' said the lady who dealt with me. 'That will be 989,000 lei please.' About 35 to 40 dollars.

'Can I give you a credit card for that?'

'No, you pay only with cash. In lei. You can change money over there.' She pointed across the room to an exchange bureau.

I went over and waved 40 dollars hopefully at the person behind the desk. 'Can I change this for lei, please?'

'No. You are buying train ticket. I can only change money if you are buying airline ticket.' She pointed at an empty chair next to her, about three feet away. 'She change money for train tickets.'

Well, she might, if she was actually there. 'Can't you move to her seat and do it?'

'No, is not possible. I only change money for airline tickets.'

Oh, come on. 'Why can't you do it? You don't look very busy to me.' By now the other three customers had gone.

'No, you must wait till she come back.'

'When will that be?'

'Monday.'

Attractive as the prospect of a weekend camping out in the booking hall was, I thought it would save time if I went to a hotel and changed money there. Telling the person on the train counter that, with luck, I might be back to complete our transaction in as little as fifteen minutes, I went into the smart, $150 per-room-per-night hotel round the corner and asked if I could change some dollars, and if so, whether it was then OK with them if I bought a train ticket with the money.

'We cannot change money here. We have no facilities,' said the blonde ice-maiden on reception. Yesterday at the airport they'd literally been falling over themselves to get to me and my dollars. Today no one seemed to want to know.

'You wait here,' said her uniformed bellboy sidekick. He came out from behind the desk, went through the glass revolving door onto the street, shook hands with a departing guest getting into the back of a waiting black limo, looked up and down the street and whistled loudly. Quicker than you could say 'pirated top-title DVD' a change-dollars-with-me spiv entered the sumptuously marbled lobby of the hotel. He was wearing a shabby V-neck pullover, dangled a fag out of one corner of his mouth, and whipped out a massive wad of lei from his back pocket when he saw me. The receptionist looked at him with very evident distaste. I wondered briefly why I never met any platinum-blonde black market currency dealers.

The bellboy grinned at me. 'Now you change money,' he said.

Bucharest houses Ceaucescu's so-called 'Parliament Palace', the second biggest building in the world after the Pentagon. He bulldozed entire neighbourhoods after a 1977 earthquake, including old churches, historic monuments, and the houses of tens of thousands of people who were then compulsorily resettled. After over a decade of largely slave labour, the Palace was virtually finished by Christmas 1989, just in time for Ceaucescu to be overthrown and executed. He had employed 270 architects, headed by a 26-year old woman who happened to have the same name as his wife. The 6km long Bulevardul Unirii, which leads up to the Palace, was deliberately built to be wider than the Champs Elysees on which it is modelled. I just stared. Constructed on higher ground than the buildings around it, the effect the Palace makes when you first see it is overwhelming.

I FINISH EARLY, TODAY IS FOOTBALL

'You want, I have woman for you.'

'I beg your pardon?' Another spiv had seen me take a photo and had appeared alongside me.

'You want lady tonight? You want see Palace? Or you want go to football tonight? You come with me, I get tickets. You change dollars with me.' So it was business as usual in this part of town then. He pointed to a ramshackle concrete building beyond the Palace, and tried to pretend that it housed the Palace ticket office. He and I walked on, with me stopping now and again to get rid of him and him making hand signals to his spiv chums over the road that he was on the case. I went past the guardhouse, where the police were more interested in the stray dogs than me, and up to the main entrance. Only then did the spiv leave me alone.

They'd had to whistle up a few more Italian-speaking guides for today's tours, most of which seemed to be for people wearing AC Milan scarves. Eventually an English-speaking party was put together comprising four Israelis, me, and a Romanian-American called Mike who'd escaped from Ceaucescu's regime in 1986, when he was 20. We set off round the deserted building. Inside the Palace, it's all marble, oak, echoing conference rooms, thick carpets and huge chandeliers. Outside, it's all street dogs, slabs of concrete and I-have-woman-for-you.

Afterwards I walked a block or so back towards the centre with Mike, who told me he was hoping to get to the game tonight as well. Romania had to win it to stay in second place in their group, while Italy had to win to stay top. Life would be difficult for the Romanian team if they lost, as they could only remain in contention if Hungary slipped up in Budapest tonight against the bottom-placed team, Lithuania, who'd been walloped at home 6-1 by Hungary back in October. The likelihood of Hungary dropping points didn't seem very high. I said goodbye to Mike, who was collected by a carload of relatives, and went back to the hotel.

Romeo arrived, in his car, half an hour late, but that was my fault because I'd sent him to the wrong hotel, which probably explained why there weren't any prostituates at mine, and he'd had to work out where I really was from what he remembered of the street address. The first thing we did was go and have a drink. If that sounds a typically East European thing to do, bear in mind that drink-driving is absolutely out in Romania, not like in Britain, where one drink or so is thought to be OK. So it was cokes and fantas all round.

Romeo was his country's answer to Statto. He presented me with an original edition of his own work, the *Enciclopedia Fotbalului Romanesc*; not just the results, but often also the attendances, dates, referees, kick-off times, stadiums and teamsheets of just about every significant game played in the country since football's humble beginnings there in about 1909. Obviously, international fixtures were included. Remember Romania's epic 23 March 1994 clash with Northern Ireland in Belfast? You don't? Try and keep up. Northern Ireland won it 2-0, in front of a Welsh referee, with Jimmy Quinn winning his 38th cap - although, as I'm sure you now remember, he was substituted by Iain Dowie after 76 minutes. Romeo had spent probably years of his life getting his data from unpromising, dusty libraries, and I'd be surprised if the result wasn't the most comprehensive volume of its kind in the country. It was probably fair to say he liked football.

We finished our third fantas and left. His car had seen better days, and was liberally decorated with patron-saint-of-car-crashes-type icons, but it was now working. Romeo suggested he show me some of the other main stadiums in Bucharest before we headed for Ghencea, perhaps realising that there were still four hours to go until kick-off and there's only so many fantas a man can drink. First stop was the Dinamo Bucharest stadium, red and white plastic bucket seats built into the side of a hill. Dinamo were the police and interior ministry team under the Communists, and thus were the most loathed club in the country. It's the same way even now. Steaua Bucharest were nearly as unpopular, because of the way nearly everybody else's new talent was regularly poached and drafted into their ranks, but they never rivalled Dinamo for the 'Chief Toadies to the Regime' title. Romeo said that even ten, twelve years on from the 'changes', he could never support Dinamo. Nowadays, virulent 'Dogs Of War' graffiti cover the wall inside the Dinamo stadium main gate. It was 6pm, and the place was virtually empty apart from a few youths doing stretching exercises against a big mower by the corner flag.

Next stop was Cotroceni stadium, scene of last night's Under-21 match. But Bucharest was not Romeo's home city, and he got lost several times on the way there. He would be a leading candidate for the title of Romania's Most Considerate Driver, and as he didn't really know the way, progress was slow and regularly punctuated by what he did know about, which was bet-you-didn't-know-that footy stats. More frequent still were loud blasts on the horn from not so considerate Balkan drivers - in other words everyone else on the road, who wanted to let him know what they thought of being held up.

After a leisurely tour of three more suburbs where Cotroceni stadium wasn't to be found, and a number-of-shots-on-goal comparison between Barcelona and Steaua in their 1986 European Cup Final clash, Romeo stopped to ask the way from a couple of teenage lads hanging round a lock-up garage. He'd struck lucky - the Cotroceni stadium was in the next street. It would probably have held 15,000 people, but I'd seen on the TV that the crowd at the Under-21 game was well under 1,000. The whole place was completely dwarfed by further towering, concrete Government megaliths from the 1970s and 80s. It felt as if the stadium planners had gone out of their way to create an atmosphere at once soul-destroying and intimidating. Boy, had they succeeded.

We moved on again. Romeo thought a friend of his would probably be going to the game as well, so as the daylight faded we stopped by at his flat to say hello and offer him a lift. His friend wasn't at home, but we met his son on the steps to the apartment block where they lived, and we went in briefly. Through the half-open door of the living room of their eighth-floor flat, I could see the hand of a probable grandparent who was watching television, motionless, in an armchair. Romeo, his friend's son and I stood in the hallway for a few minutes while Romeo finished off a statistical review, for my benefit, of Steaua's 1986 win while the lad's teenage sister got ready to head off to a party. We were deep into the second half of the final by now. The inspired second-half (after 73 minutes to be precise) substitution of veteran campaigner Anghel Iordanescu had thrown Barcelona off their stride, and a technically inferior Steaua team had kept the Catalans out until the end of extra time and into the penalty shootout. Lacatus and Balint won it for Steaua from the spot. Like England's 1966 World Cup win, in Romania the memory of Steaua's 1986 triumph is kept very much alive to this day. And thanks to money, it will be decades before teams like Steaua, or any club from outside the top four or five European countries, can again compete on level terms in what the European Cup has become.

The fantas had hit bottom, so I went to their bathroom. I didn't really know who these people were, only that I would never be able to find the street where they lived again; but for a minute or so I was able to examine the family's choice of toothpaste and investigate their laundry drying over the bath. The tiny, high window looked out over darkened rooftops and chimney stacks, and through the net curtains of the flats across the courtyard, I could see the shapes of one or two people moving about. Two minutes later I was out of the building and walking away.

On the way back to the car, Romeo asked a man with a dog (this one actually seemed to have an owner) for directions to the Ghencea stadium. After driving for a minute or two, it became obvious that the man might have been right about the general direction we had to follow, but had been somewhat shaky about the detail. The traffic was now even busier, it was now dark, and before long Romeo was evidently driving along just hoping for the best. At this point, however, we began to notice cars with Romanian flags hanging out the boot or the side window, each with several Steaua-scarved, baseball-capped, bomber-jacketed lads inside. I figured there was more than an outside chance that these people were going to the game. So I suggested to Romeo that he pick a car and follow it.

With hindsight, this was definitely a bad idea. From being almost hesitant at the wheel, Romeo suddenly began to drive like the hindmost charioteer at the Circus Maximus when they've let the lions in too early. The fans he chose to follow were in a much more powerful car than us and shot off into the far distance at every set of lights, leaving him with the job of cutting everyone up something appalling if we were to make up the lost ground. For several blocks we just about kept in touch, at high cost to his brakes and tyres, as we were to discover later that night. To fill in the idle moments of the chase, Romeo wound the clock back another 26 years from Steaua's triumph and began listing the goalscorers in the classic 1960 Real Madrid-Eintracht Frankfurt European Cup Final. The game finished 7-3, and even Romeo struggled for a while to remember who put the cross in for the third German goal.

What seemed like only three lifetimes later, we saw the glow from the Ghencea stadium floodlights and Romeo looked for somewhere to park. All kerb spaces were taken, but the pavements were still unoccupied, so he shooed some pedestrians out the way and left it there. We set off on foot to do the last mile or so to the stadium, looking for something to eat as we went. Dinner turned out to be a sticky bun filled with synthetic cream in a plastic pack, bought from a stall by a tram-stop that sold the usual East European everyday necessities: fags, cheap watches, lottery and bus tickets, lukewarm fantas (not again, thanks), porn mags and twelve types of vodka.

There were three security rings around the stadium, but the first one was just to ensure you held a ticket. After that, the gathering crowds set off down a long road, only lit indirectly by the stadium floodlights, past a factory to the main entrance. Beyond the second security check, no liquid of any kind was permitted, not even water. Inside the stadium perimeter, no drink or even food was being sold apart from sunflower and pumpkin seeds, presumably officially sanctioned on the grounds of being fairly harmless. Sunflower seeds are Romania's equivalent of popcorn. Way before kick-off, all the stands were ankle deep in seed shells. It felt like a budgie cage as you waded along to find your seat.

Emerich Jenei, Steaua's 1986 coach and thus a revered figure in the national game, was being interviewed on TV on the steps of the main stand, while what looked like the entire police force and half the army had set up camp on the open ground just behind the stadium. At the third security point - the steps to each block in the stadium - police in combat fatigues examined everyone's ticket minutely.

The security seemed a bit over the top, as there was no alcohol to be had, not an Italian in sight until just before the start, and an upbeat atmosphere created by the locals. Perhaps this was simply old habits dying hard. Here was a big football match where thousands of people would gather. For decades until 1989, and arguably ever since then as well, large crowds spelt potential for civil unrest, and so you kept the upper hand by wheeling out the full state machinery of crowd control. It didn't matter who the (footballing) opposition were, since it was your own people who had to be kept in line.

It was only 8pm, still 90 minutes before kick-off, but the stadium was full. Romeo told me that Ghencea is the national side's favourite stadium, rather than the 'official', and larger, Lia Manoliu National Stadium across the city, because of the atmosphere the crowd generates. As so often, this has a lot to do with the absence of an athletics track round the playing area at Ghencea: the spectators are right up there next to the action. Tonight the pitch looked in pretty poor shape, muddy and still waterlogged from the winter. It was bound to have a bearing on the game, helping to level out any skill difference between the sides.

We had seats behind the goal, just in front of a group of locals in Saxon helmets, facepaint and fake blond pigtails: in Transylvania, in western Romania, German is still widely understood and spoken. They were getting in the mood. 'Romania, Romania, Ole, Ole, Ole,' they sang, in between mouthfuls of sunflower seeds. 'Good Evening Italy, Good Luck Romania', said the fair-minded operators of the electronic scoreboard, while the aficionados behind the goal at the other end unfurled the biggest flag I'd yet seen, half the width of the pitch, covering the first twenty rows of spectators and putting the Polish effort in Lodz into the shade. We had flags at our end too, little hand-held efforts like the ones you wave when the Queen goes by. 10-year old kids smoked. Right behind them, soldiers sat on the steps blocking the exits.

I FINISH EARLY, TODAY IS FOOTBALL

9.30 came round. Demonstrating solidarity with home fans just about everywhere, this 24,000 crowd booed all the Italian players' names while cheering their own to the rafters. My airport taxi driver had been pretty accurate about the make-up of the Romanian side, but he had got one thing round his ear: Moldovan was not 'finish', he was playing. And also, encouragingly for the home team, Adrian Ilie was playing his first game for two months, having been injured early on in the season for his club, Valencia. But there was inexperience too: five players from the Romanian Under-21 squad had been picked by Boloni, the national coach, for tonight's game. This was something of a risky, untried, experimental team he was fielding against one of the top three or four national sides in Europe.

There weren't more than a couple of hundred Italians to be seen: either Bucharest wasn't high on their list of fun places to visit, for some reason, or they were all still tangling with the spivs around the Parliament Palace. They didn't get in until very near the kick-off. Penned into a little section by one of the corner flags, they were still the biggest contingent of visiting fans I'd seen so far, large enough for the locals to identify them and supply some suitable verbal abuse.

'Which visiting national team never lost at Wembley?' asked Romeo with a grin. You could have knocked me down with a replica kit top, but the answer turned out to be Romania. After Marcin in Poland and Hakan in Norway, Romeo thus became the third person I'd met to impress on me just how well their country's team or players had performed against England at Wembley. I'd done nothing to provoke these people into rubbing it in like this. You'd almost think the Home of Football was significant to them.

The teams came out and we got under way. 'This is the thirteenth meeting between these two sides,' said Romeo in finest John Motson mode. 'Of the twelve games so far, Romania have won two, drawn two, and lost eight.' So now I knew.

On paper, here were two top sides, both quarter-finalists less than nine months previously at Euro 2000. But it hadn't been a good spell for Romania since then. They'd struggled to beat Lithuania at home in September, and had gone down 3-0 to Italy in

Milan a month later, in what was presumably the twelfth meeting between the two sides. Tonight the gulf in class soon became apparent, but because of the pitch the Italians were having trouble making their superiority count and Romania went close to scoring several times early on. The crowd got behind them, and even the corporate suits in the main stand joined in the Mexican waves. An early Italian goal was disallowed for offside, and the fans near us took the opportunity to gesticulate and yell something like 'Bad luck chaps, better luck next time' at the Italian fans in the corner.

After half an hour, Inzaghi got away a shot which was deflected past Bogdan Stelea in the Romanian goal. That owed a lot to chance, but four minutes later came the best piece of skill of the night, a fantastic Inzaghi run, a one-two with Del Piero and no chance for the keeper. 2-0 before half time and the Romanians couldn't find a way back. The second half lacked the incident of the first, with the Italians more than content with what they had. This was their trickiest away tie in this group, and all three points looked to be safely in the can. There was no point attempting anything fancy. This was, after all, Italy with a two-goal lead.

But there was consolation for the locals as the game ended. The man on the PA relished the job of telling the crowd that in Budapest, plucky Lithuania had held Hungary to a 1-1 draw. A Romanian win in Georgia the following Wednesday would still leave them with a good chance of second place in the group, if they could beat Hungary on 2 June. Maybe Boloni needed to coax Hagi out of his retirement, which, unlike Petrescu's, seemed to be self-imposed.

Thanks to BMWs parked on the main walkways, it took half an hour to get out of the stadium. It was a disappointing result for the locals, and for the only neutral - me. Romeo and I each had a Big Mac to cheer ourselves up after walking back to the car. When we found it again we realised that the major pothole Romeo had clipped earlier that night, as he attempted to stay in touch with the racing Steaua fans, had done some serious damage - the tyre was flat. It was now half past midnight. Neither of us really knew where in the city we were and, wherever it was, for a moment or two I thought we might be staying there. However, Romeo was an unflappable lad and had come prepared - he had a spare and it was well inflated. 'We eat first,' he said, maintaining an impressive sense of priorities. So we demolished the burgers and then set about the wheel. In 15 minutes we were mobile again. But the police had erected barriers on the road we needed to take, meaning we would have to set off in the wrong direction entirely, taking us further away from the parts of the city we knew, with no flag-waving cars or stadium floodlights (or lights of any other kind - Bucharest doesn't really do street lamps) to use as navigational aids.

No problem to Romeo. If you can't get through a barrier on a Romanian road you find a way round it, even if it means heading off across non-traditional driving surfaces. Romeo showed a well-honed aptitude for driving along housing estate walkways, bulldozing through narrow gaps in hedges and bouncing across pavements until we reached the road a few yards round the corner from where the police had blocked it. About 1.30am he dropped me off at my hotel, which at least was on the main road north to Ploiesti, his home town, so he had a chance of getting back before daybreak, assuming no further tyre blowouts.

I would have struggled to get to see this game without his help. Thanking him once again, I said I hoped he'd enjoy the video of Manchester United highlights I'd given him. I know some might regard such a gift as an odd way of saying thank you to someone who's helped you, but Romeo had said he was a fan of Sir Alex's team. It was of course very unexpected to find a United fan in a country like Romania. Mostly, their fans don't live as close to Manchester as that.

The next night I got the train to Sofia, as it was on my way to Athens. I'd spent Sunday seeing what remained of the sights and dodging sundry offers of prostitutes and black market currency deals. The train conductor was drunk and asleep when I got on board, but he was then woken by the only other traveller besides me. At the border, the Romanians stalked off with my passport for 20 minutes, only to give it back without a word, but the Bulgarians were much more friendly ('Englishman!') than I expected at 2 am Then I was left in peace.

YOU COME WITH ME - I GET TICKETS

After Romania, Bulgaria seemed about as threatening and stressful as a week in the Seychelles. The spiv count was well down - one or two in the main station, who were caught on the hop as they weren't expecting a Westerner to get off a train from Bucharest, but otherwise I found I could walk down the street for as much as 100 yards at a time without being offered any women, massages, cheap, mechanically-reliable taxis or favourable exchange rates.

It was now Monday, and I had a flight from here early on Wednesday to Athens, for the game in England's group that night between Greece and Germany. So with a free day on Tuesday, I hired a guide to take me to Rila, the country's most famous monastery, up in the mountains about 80 miles, and four different bus rides, south of Sofia. The guide turned up with a driver and a car. This was a bit grander than my usual way of doing things, but I couldn't face more Balkan public transport just then, and it was only for a day. I explained to Karina, the guide, why I was here, and she remembered that when England last played Bulgaria in summer 1999, she'd done a tour of Sofia for a group of visiting fans. She'd been apprehensive at the prospect, being well aware of English fans' overseas reputation. But they turned out to be from the official England fan club, and each one gave her a red rose at the end of the tour. The big softies.

Next morning my flight to Athens wasn't listed when I got to the airport. 'Balkan Airlines suspended their flights six weeks ago,' said the person at the information desk. 'That flight didn't go yesterday, it won't go today and it won't go tomorrow. Welcome to Sofia, get to know it,' she said, at least giving me a smile. 'You're stuck here.'

8.

No, You Must Pay Cash

Greece - Germany, Spiros Louis Olympic Stadium, Athens, Wednesday 28 March 2001

'YOUR ONLY CHANCE is to go back to the airport and hope for a no-show.'

I was in Sofia, but I didn't want to be. I was meant to be on a flight to Athens, taking off about now, but Balkan Airlines had gone bust and wouldn't be taking off anywhere, probably ever again. In the downtown office of Greece's national airline, Olympic Airways, the assistant had just told me that their Sofia-Athens flights were full until after Easter. It wasn't looking good: I was stranded in Bulgaria, with nothing to fall back on but a valid Mastercard (albeit one with a generous and largely unused high four-figure credit limit). And tonight's big Greece-Germany Group 9 clash could be set to kick off at the Red Planet Stadium on Mars for all my chances of being there. I didn't even have a match ticket.

There was a flight to Tirana this afternoon from Sofia. England were playing Albania that night, and for a wild half minute or so while waiting in the Olympic office I thought about that - I wouldn't have needed a visa. But getting away again might have been more of a problem, at least for the wallet, than getting in.

'There's no point in me putting you on the waiting list,' continued the assistant at the Olympic office. 'There's a dozen other people I'd have to call first. But they won't all go to the airport. If you really want to fly, get back to the airport and let them know you're there.'

I left the office, and walked a few blocks to the ambitiously named Perfekt Café and thought through my options. The café was next to the new city centre metro station, and teams of workmen were laying a new patio just outside. The place was almost empty, so the staff were keeping themselves entertained by playing heavy metal videos, although that could have been the noise of the power tools being used outside.

I wasn't sure what to do. I could try to get on the Olympic flight, and pick up my original plans from there. Or I could cut my losses, hang around in Sofia for tonight's Bulgaria-Northern Ireland game, and come back with British Airways the day after. The only problems were minor ones; nothing more serious than not having a ticket for either game or a ticket for either flight.

My efforts from back in the UK to establish contact with the Panathinaikos, hold on, let me get this right, 'Mad Boys' fan club, in the hope that one of them would get me a ticket, had got nowhere. Neither had a more conventional approach direct to the Olympiakos club. Germany were a powerful attraction in Athens - much more so than Northern Ireland in Sofia, all in all - and so there was a good chance that the Germany game would be a sell-out. Dollars wouldn't exercise the same leverage for me in Athens that they had done in Bucharest the previous Saturday, so getting a black market ticket might not be easy. Plenty of room for cock-ups there then, I thought as I ordered another ice cream and coke. I'll stick around in Sofia, pay up for a BA ticket, and try and get it back on the insurance. And this vanilla ice cream is fantastic.

Then they turned off the heavy metal and put on a Beatles CD. The Fab Four just don't do it for me, so I left the cafe and tried to leave the country. Athens it was.

The Olympic office at the airport was upstairs from the departure hall. When I got there, two cats were sleeping on the window sill and the manager was at her desk. I gave her my name and she told me that they would know whether they could fit me in at about 1.30, which was still nearly two hours away. I got a coffee downstairs and started to wait.

There were only about 15 flights a day from this airport, but for some reason five of them took off in a 20 minute period in the early afternoon, so the place started to fill up around midday. I was very tempted to go round telling people that Athens was an overrated place, and that for history, culture and food they'd be much better off going to Tirana or Warsaw instead. The lines at check-in were longest for Frankfurt, which cheered me up a bit.

It was after 1pm so I went back up to the office to make a nuisance of myself again. The boss had gone, to be replaced by someone else, shooting the breeze with three people who looked like lifelong friends of his. All of them were chainsmoking and the cats had gone outside. He didn't look that interested in helping anyone fly anywhere. When he finally deigned to lift an eyebrow at me to ask what I wanted, he told me to go back to check-in, where I found the manager I'd originally spoken to. She told me there was a seat for me, but that I had to pay $150 cash, in dollars or lev, the Bulgarian currency.

I wasn't carrying that sort of money, not in cash anyway.

'Do you take a credit card?' I asked in a semi-panic. To have got a last-minute seat on the aircraft but be refused it because I couldn't rustle up enough cash on the spot wasn't a happy prospect. If I couldn't pay by credit card, maybe Olympic Airways would accept coloured beads, cattle or exotic oriental spices as payment instead.

'No, you must pay cash.' She pointed through the revolving doors. 'There is an ATM inside the Customs Building across the car park.'

Inside the Customs Building. Of course. Where else would you put the one and only ATM at an international airport in a European capital city? I got the lev and five minutes later I had a single ticket to Athens in my hand. I even had a choice of smoking or non.

The incoming Olympic flight was late. An hour late. I was just thinking again that the game was up when I heard that the flight lasted only one hour, not two as on my original Balkan Airlines schedule. So the end result was the same. I hadn't been able to find out the kick-off time before leaving England, but even if it was early for a weekday fixture, such as 6pm, I'd probably make it. Ticketless maybe, but I'd be there or thereabouts. And if I couldn't get a ticket, I could always find a bar to watch the game in.

YOU COME WITH ME - I GET TICKETS

Vassilis climbed over me and into his window seat. Both of his pieces of hand luggage were bigger than my one bag. The overhead lockers were so full that he had to put one bag between his feet, and squash the other one down by sitting on top of it, an arrangement which the cabin crew seemed to accept as normal. We were in the air shortly before 4 o'clock, seven hours later than I would have been had Balkan not gone belly up, and once we'd levelled out the cabin attendant handed out newspapers in Greek and Bulgarian. Neither of these were much good to me. Vassilis grabbed a Greek one, and turned straight to the back page. Greek newspapers are no different to British ones in terms of where to look for the sports coverage. Evidently he was a man with a mission, possibly even the same mission as me.

'6pm,' he said in English. He must have noticed the English paperback I was reading. But how did he know I cared about the kick-off time? Was he telepathic as well as observant?

I leaned across to look. 'Is that the football?' I asked. Doubtfully, because although my Greek isn't too good, I did know you don't play football in shoes like the ones in the picture he was looking at. Not internationally, anyway.

'No, the basketball. It's the European Cup semi-final tonight, against Alaves, from Spain. I'm a season ticket holder. If we're not delayed any more, I can do it.'

A kindred spirit. I explained to him just how precisely I understood his problem. 'What time is the football, then?'

He turned back one page, then another. Today at least, basketball was clearly bigger news in Greece than football. '9.30pm,' he said.

9.30. Same kick-off time as in Bucharest for the Italy game I was at last weekend. For me, the disaster of Balkan Airlines' collapse was turning into a piece of quite enjoyable cake. There would be time not just to find the hotel I'd booked into from England, but to settle in, get a shower and a meal, head slowly over to the ground and somehow get a ticket. Now I'd got a plane ticket, I was sure I'd be able to get a match ticket. If it wasn't a sellout, no problem; and if it was, there would be touts. Greek police spooked me marginally less than Romanian ones did. I sat back and relaxed for the first time since the Perfekt Café. Wasn't the Balkan attitude to time wonderful? Why rush and play the game at 6 when you can hang around until 9.30?

Vassilis was clearly a mine of useful information. 'Are there any tickets left for tonight?' I asked him.

'For the football? Thousands. For the basketball, no chance.'

Vassilis had the same outlook as many English fans on the club versus country debate. For him, country came a long way behind club in importance, whatever the sport. His wife thought he was crazy on that one, but to him it was all part of supporting your club properly. He also thought I was talking outdated sentimental tosh when I said it was dull how a few rich Western European clubs had come to dominate the later stages of club competitions like the Champions' League. 'Be realistic - that's where the money is,' he said. 'It's always going to be like that from now.'

He told me he ran a company in Varna, on Bulgaria's Black Sea coast, and that he often travelled to the UK, as his business had contacts in north Yorkshire. He was well clued up on Leeds' progress in the 2000-01 Champions' League. Remember Leeds in the Champions' League?

We landed at nearly 5pm local time, and Vassilis didn't hang around. Kick-off, or whatever basketball players do to start a game, was in just over an hour, in an arena most of the way across the city. As his bags already filled half the cabin, he had nothing in the hold and could run straight through the arrivals hall.

As for me, two minutes later I was heading into Athens in a new, pillar-box red Golf VR6, with the roof open and Eminem on the stereo, driven by a girl with jet black hair, shades, a tight blouse and spray-on white trousers. It was about seventy-five degrees, the palm trees flashed by and the Mediterranean shimmered in the late afternoon sun beyond. OK, so it was Vassilis' wife's car, Vassilis having very kindly offered me a lift into the city, or at least as far along their route as the end station on the new Athens metro, and I was slumming it in the back, trying to make space to sit among several weeks' worth of carrier bags, blankets, clothes and discarded hamburger boxes while Vassilis frantically searched the glove box and everywhere else within reach for his basketball season ticket. It wasn't there. We stopped first at their house, and then at his father's house a couple of streets further on, while he raced in to look for it. He was gone a few minutes, taking the chance in his dad's house for a quick shower and change of clothes.

He got back in wearing a polo shirt in yellow, his club's colour. It wasn't yet 5.30, he'd found his ticket, and he had time to chill out a bit. Georgia, his wife, spoke excellent English as well: she ran a hotel in the city. They were a very high energy couple who, perhaps because they hadn't seen each other for a few days, both talked simultaneously more or less the whole way into the city, often in English for my benefit, which took consideration for visitors further than they probably had to. After a while we were talking about Bulgaria and the swankier nightclubs in Black Sea coastal cities like Varna, where Vassilis' business was.

'They're all mafia run,' Vassilis told me, to my not very great surprise. 'The bouncers say, "If you've got a gun, you must leave it with us. If you haven't got a gun, kindly go and get one as soon as possible. Then leave it with us".'

They dropped me at the last stop on the amazing new metro, which is cool, clean, quick, cheap and efficient. I'd studied their well-thumbed, mayonnaise-smeared Athens A-Z (Alpha to Omega in fact) in the car and remembered enough from that to cover the ten minute walk to my hotel from the nearest metro station. I did what Vassilis did: I had a shower, got changed, and headed for the stadium.

I was two hours early but the metro was full of fans on their way out to the north-eastern suburb where the Olympic Stadium was. I was putting my trust in Vassilis' assertion that there would be plenty of tickets, though I couldn't ignore a nagging feeling that as he'd clearly been out the country for a while up until today, what had been true about tickets when he'd left for Bulgaria might no longer apply tonight. Germans and Greeks mingled happily on the train, though if I'd been a native and felt like asserting that my team's footballing skills were the more developed and that victory was therefore already in the bag, I might have thought twice about making an issue of it with the particular group of five large Germans who got on near me.

NO, YOU MUST PAY CASH

At the metro stop for the stadium, the police assumed I was German, which came as a shock initially, but in the circumstances was fair enough, as I don't look very Greek. Talking English didn't make any difference, as they must simply have thought, OK, here's another German using his English to talk to us. So I was told to wait around a bit, as a police escort would soon round up all the Germans from the last metro train and march them to the stadium, helmets, batons, shields and all. And that was nothing, you should have seen what the police were equipped with.

As we neared the stadium itself I lost the escort and started asking around about tickets. Somebody pointed me to a portakabin the other side of another police line, where it turned out that although I might have slipped the escort, I was back in German-occupied territory. The ticket I bought (and Vassilis, you were right, there were thousands) was in a block earmarked for the travelling German support.

This was bad news. I would now have to sing the German national anthem, cheer any German goals and, to add possible injury to unintentional insult, then risk having sharp, pointy objects thrown at me afterwards by disgruntled locals if, as expected, the Germans won. And what made it even worse of course was that Germany were in England's group, and England were hoping the Greeks would do them a favour tonight and take a couple of points off them, or ideally all three.

I'd eaten the mandatory in-country hot dog at the metro station, so I went to sit on a low wall and hummed Deutschland, Deutschland Uber Alles to myself. Despite having to pretend to be a German, I was feeling pretty chuffed right now, because for most of the morning I hadn't thought I would even get to Greece, let alone to a numbered seat inside the Olympic Stadium. But it had all come right, and my 100% record of getting in to see the games I'd travelled to was intact. And anyway, maybe it was about time to see things from the away fans' perspective.

You couldn't get anything else to eat or drink, so people were just hanging around outside the steps for whatever sector their seat was in. I was reading an interview with Rudi Voeller in the match programme (printed in Greek and English, which I bet went down well with tonight's away fans) when four people in various types of entirely black Eintracht Frankfurt replica kit came and sat on the wall next to me. The metal studs on their jackets spelt out the words 'Eiserne Adler' - 'Iron Eagles.'

I got talking to a couple of them. One was about six foot three and worked as a journalist for a heavy metal magazine, while the other was about six foot four, thought that the best sport ever to have been invented in England was speedway, and had tasteful Viking-type crossed swords on his enormous belt buckle. They were called Sven Wiese and Buffo Schnaedelbach, and within minutes they'd each given me their business cards and invited me and my whole family to north Germany's premier outdoor Ozzfest-type heavy metal event at Wacken, just outside Hamburg. Apparently a sedate, sensibly haircutted, Pringle-sweatered electronic beat combo called Helloween were to be the 2001 headline attraction. After a week of bankrupt Bulgarian airlines, aggressive Romanian spivs and train tickets costing almost a million lei in scruffy banknotes for a one way ride, it was good to be back among such ordinary, everyday people as Sven and Buffo. Both of them seemed to have spent a lot of time in England watching football, such as the Bradford-Newcastle game the previous January.

'We spent £21 each to get in at QPR and the view was crap,' announced Buffo in alarmingly idiomatic English. Having twice been to Loftus Road myself I had to agree. They weren't that impressed with Leyton Orient's ground either. As for Wembley, Sven's memories of the place went back 20 years to the big clashes of 1981 featuring Ipswich, which he'd gone along to with his dad. As far as I could recall, Ipswich had a pretty rough time in the post-Bobby Robson 1980s, and I certainly didn't remember them playing at Wembley any time in 1981, which will go down in musical history as the year of the classic Tottingham Hotspur Cup Final number, 'Ossie's Going to Wembley, His Knees Have Gone All Trembly, La la la la, La la la la.' But it turned out that Sven didn't mean football at all. He meant the well-known Ipswich Witches, for whom lots of big Danish blokes ride very noisy motorbikes in circles and have names like, well, Sven.

NO, YOU MUST PAY CASH

As for tonight, they said they'd be happy with a 1-1. Germany, as I didn't need reminding, were already runaway leaders of Group 9, five points clear of England, who'd at last got under way at the weekend with a win over Finland at Anfield, with the winning goal scored by David Beckham in front of his many admirers in the Kop. With that kind of lead, Sven thought it wouldn't be a disaster if Germany dropped a couple of points away from home this evening.

There were now about 45 minutes or so to kick-off. A respectable number of Germans were here, of both sexes and all ages, but not nearly as many as they'd had tickets allocated. They were going to have to make a lot of noise to be heard. We couldn't see the Greek fans arriving, as they were being carefully kept away from us. And the stadium was massive, capacity 75,000 and destined to be the main athletics venue for the 2004 Olympics. 'Only a thousand German fans will travel today,' said Buffo. '1,500, maximum. It's midweek, and for us this isn't a fixture with the history that games with England have got.' I didn't think he was saying that just to please me, I think he really meant it. In those pre-Munich 5-1 days, it was somehow encouraging to feel that even though they'd lost to us only once since 1966, England-Germany fixtures still meant as much to the Germans as they did to us.

We flicked through tonight's match programme. As always with publications like this, it tried to build up the game as just the latest in a series of epic encounters involving the two countries. But it must have been tough going for the compilers. Before tonight, Germany and Greece, or Hellas as they more correctly call themselves, had met seven times since 1960. Unfortunately, as the programme rather sheepishly admitted, 'Hellas has never won Germany'. Not unless you counted two wins against the former East Germany, which you could read about in a slightly condescending little box at the bottom of page 13. But twelve years after the Wall came down, probably even the Ossies (former East Germans that is, not 1981 Tottingham's Ossie) in the crowd didn't count those.

YOU COME WITH ME - I GET TICKETS

Sven and Buffo had tickets in another sector, so we said auf wiedersehen, till we met again some muddy day in a field outside Hamburg within ear-splitting distance of a giant loudspeaker stack. As I took my seat, teams of mountaineering German fans were climbing all over the concrete supports for the tier above putting up banners. 'Ruhrpott Rambos,' said one. 'Tarzan Borussia Moenchengladbach,' proclaimed another. Tarzan? Hmm. In the 1970s, maybe. But I guess Borussia have to trade on old glories. Today's more accurate 'Tiddles Borussia Moenchengladbach' just wouldn't sound as fearsome. Half the space on a Trier FC banner was given over to announcing that they were a second division team, which seemed a somewhat un-German thing to draw attention to. And the downbeat theme continued. The Trier banner was right there alongside one for the so-called 'Cologne Underdogs'. To an outsider, it all looked a bit apologetic and defeatist. Suddenly Buffo's predicted 1-1 was looking like one of the more optimistic forecasts.

Once the red-plumed Greek marching band had finally moved off the centre circle to the touchline, the game could get under way. All my instincts told me to support Greece. You'd have to, wouldn't you, with a choice between them and Germany? But at the time, and however laughable it seems in hindsight, you could make a case for a German win playing into English hands: Greece looked like England's main rivals for the Group Nine play-off spot which, with just four points from a possible nine, seemed just then to be the limit of England's ambitions. So when Rehmer made it 1-0 after only six minutes, I didn't get the usual sinking feeling that there is when Germany score.

Despite the powerful counter-attraction of the basketball half a mile down the road, there were 53,000 people here tonight. Almost 52,000 of them were Greek, so when they levelled it a quarter of an hour later, it was bedlam. Rockets, flares, smoke, fireworks, horns; you name it, the local fans had brought it and were sending it up in flames. There was almost as much noise, in protest, four minutes later when the Portuguese ref pointed to the spot for a German penalty. That made it 2-1 to Germany until the stroke of half time, when Georgiadis levelled it again.

NO, YOU MUST PAY CASH

Except I didn't see the goal because I was too busy people-watching. 1,000 German fans were singing and yelling 'Deutschland, Deutschland!', 'Stand tall if you're a German', and the awesome 'Ooh aah, ooh aah, Deutschland Wieder Da' ('Germany There Again'). But when Georgiadis struck they all went quiet; instantly after that it was half time, and it was 2-2. Anxious Germans all around me were asking each other for news of England's game with Albania, which had kicked off an hour earlier and so was just finishing. Hearing that England had won 3-1 didn't cheer them up. Opening my mouth to shout 'Hooray for England' or something at this point didn't seem like a good plan, so I concentrated on trying to look as Teutonic as possible. You had the feeling suddenly that maybe a draw wouldn't be good enough for Germany after all. It was a young and inexperienced team that Rudi Voeller had at that stage, a team which had needed an 88th minute goal by a substitute, who was universally deemed to have been offside at the time, to scrape past Albania in Germany the previous Saturday.

The second half here looked an exciting prospect, but unfortunately the Greeks went badly off the boil. Germany held them easily, even after Deisler got himself sent off after an hour for a second bookable offence. Deisler trudged off slowly and dejectedly, but you never felt that the Germans would let something as trivial as handing the Greeks a one-man advantage upset them. On came substitute Miroslav Klose after 67 minutes - he was the young lad who scored the winner against Albania, and we know all about him now after his achievements in the finals in Korea. And he did it again, putting Germany back into the lead with just eight minutes to go. Then the man on the PA, in English, said that the 'German people' would have to wait behind for 15 minutes after the game - basically so that the Greek fans could grab all the seats on the last metro trains.

In the final minute, Marko Bode, another sub, made it 4-2. The German team came over to their fans to applaud their support. Oliver Kahn yomped across and chucked his gloves and his towel into the ninth row of the stand. At the top of the steps, the Greek police were in place to keep us all back for the stipulated 15 minutes. Victorious Germans untied all their banners from the wire fences and concrete pillars. It was now past 11.30 and the metro would stop for the night soon, and everyone started to get a bit agitated. The Germans in the next block were being allowed out, but the Greek police in our sector were immovable, even though it was now over 20 minutes since the final whistle went. And then all of a sudden it was the Germans who started to defy authority by climbing over fences and ducking round pillars to get to the sector next door and its more pliant policemen. I'd had enough hanging around so I joined them. The locals seemed to have taken their defeat in pretty good heart, and there was no trouble as far as I could see. And there were extra late metro trains.

My train stopped one station short of where I needed to be, but after a quick look at someone's map I headed off in roughly the right direction for my hotel. It was well after midnight by now. A lot had happened since I'd arrived at a deserted Sofia airport at 6.45 that morning, and the day finished with me getting lost and needing to ask for directions from some drunken Bulgarians outside a very back-street Athens bar at about 1.30. Amazingly, what they told me turned out to be accurate, and I found the hotel a few minutes later. I'd need to make an early start in the morning because the check-in for my 6.30am flight back to the UK would open in three hours' time. The two ends of the night would meet in the middle soon. I got the hotel to fix me a taxi, as no buses would be running at the time I needed to get up, and the new airport (new that morning in fact; our flight from Sofia the day before had been the last ever to land at the old airport) was at least 15 miles out of town.

The taxi driver and I talked a bit about the game, which he hadn't seen because he'd been working. I wondered if that meant he'd been working the entire night, and if so what his driving skills and reactions would be like at 5am He was quite impressed to discover that although I was English, I'd come all the way to Athens to see Greece play football. I noticed he was looking at me at this point.

'I like you,' he said, with a smile. Normally when a taxi driver smiles at you and tells you he likes you and it's 5am, it's a signal to bale out of the vehicle with all available speed. Even Athens

Above: Albanian players arrive for
their match with Finland.

Below: Albanian pre-match warm-up.

Above: Ticket sales in Helsinki
- anyone need any 'lipunmyynti'?

Below: Kadriorg Stadium, Estonia;
VIPs allowed in, but no guns or poodles.

Right and below:
Estonian fans -
that's Ott
in the kilt.

Above: Estonian and Portuguese fans share an all-friends-together photo call after Portugal's 3-1 win.

Below: Vitor, Matti the referee, me, and Martin in the Vana Villemi after the game - with Roadsweeper across the top and inept cameraman to the right.

Above: Another busy moment for de Vlieger
in the Belgian goal.

Below: In Bucharest with Romeo, the stats man.

Above, left and below: Black leather, yellow pigtails and three-coloured flags: Romanian fans get in the mood for the Italy game.

Above: Romania kept out this early Italian attack,
but went down 2-0 in the end.

Below: Former Romanian dictator
Ceaucescu's Parliament Palace.

Above: It's 'Deutschland Uber Alles' night for me,
flanked by Sven, German speedway and
heavy metal fan (left), and Buffo, German
heavy metal and speedway fan (right).

Below: German banners inside
the Athens Olympic Stadium.

Another Olympic Stadium - Moscow this time:
Andrei (my 'twin'), Ilya and Aleksandr.

We're
H - A - P - P - Y,
We're
H - A - P - P - Y
... Andrei's
squaddie chum
from Ryazan -
second left (above).

Above: Iceland; just two hours till kick off in the World Cup. Another ticket is sold.

Right: Iceland; the Bulgarian squad check out Top Shop in Reykjavik.

Reykjavik: the Laugardalsvollur Stadium Megastore.

Above: Iceland - Bulgaria; 11 'ovs' against 11 'ssons',
one of them clearly thinking it's the quidditch World Cup.

Below: I am Tushansky;
Bulgarian TV interview the former star.

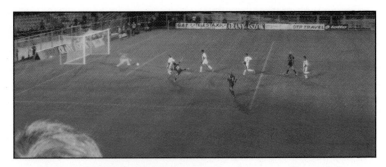

Above: Curtains for Hungary's chances; Georgia's Gocha Jamarauli gives his country a 2-1 lead.

Left: Tbilisi; Dato (l), Dima (r) and I discuss AC Milan's forthcoming season over a few 'bears'.

Below: Budapest - a scrum forms for one of those last 65,000 tickets.

Above: Tsminda Sameba church, Caucasus mountains,
near the Chechen border; 3 September 2001.

Below: Istanbul; Austria warm up, as if that were
necessary here in the Ali Sami Yen stadium.

The goals go in...

...in Helsinki

...in Athens

...in Moscow.

traffic is quiet at that time of the morning, however, so we were going along deserted expressways at nearly 60mph, which made a rapid exit seem a marginally bigger physical risk than staying put. But in fact he was just saying he appreciated the fact that I'd come to watch the game, even though it meant I'd watched his country's top footballers have four goals whacked past them at home by a team of novices reduced to ten men for half an hour.

'Because I like what you do here, I charge you fair price for this journey, 'he offered generously. I thought that was pretty good: only 12 hours in this city and already I'd earned nuff respect not to be gratuitously ripped off by its taxi drivers.

9.

You Have no Ticket? Pfffhh!

Netherlands - Cyprus, Philips Stadium, Eindhoven, Wednesday 25 April 2001

ONE OF THE MOST wince-inducing pieces of TV sports journalism I can remember, one of those reports that are physically painful to watch, was broadcast in spring 2000, just after Ruud van Nistelrooy's transfer to Manchester United was announced as being all but sealed.

Here's what happens on that report. The news camera crew are at the PSV training ground just outside Eindhoven watching the multi-million pound man train. Suddenly he lands off-balance, twists his knee inside out and down he goes. You can almost hear the wrench as the ligaments tear. He doesn't get up, and the transfer to United is on hold, possibly for ever.

It turned out that van Nistelrooy had aggravated an injury to a previously suspect knee. He underwent surgery and almost a year of rehabilitation before resuming his career in early 2001 for PSV. The goals began to rain in again, and by March or early April that year Sir Alex and assorted United bagmen were back in Holland to revive the deal. On Monday 23 April 2001, van Nistelrooy passed a medical. For a British record £19m (a figure which it took United almost two months to break by signing Seba Veron), United had got their man.

Two days later, van Nistelrooy was set to make his international comeback for Holland, against Cyprus, on his club ground in

YOU HAVE NO TICKET? PFFFHH!

Eindhoven. Dutch coach Louis van Gaal selected four strikers for the game, suggesting that maybe he was after a goal or two to boost the Netherlands' goal difference, in view of the three way fight with Portugal and the Republic of Ireland which was developing at the top of their World Cup qualifying Group. The man of the moment still lacked match fitness at top level and wouldn't be risked for the whole game, but the word was that he would come on as a sub, sometime in the second half. So one way or another, interest in the Cyprus game was enormous.

You had to feel a bit for the Cypriots. Their record in recent times hasn't been all that bad - a win against Spain a few years back in the 51st minute of the second half comes to mind (reminds you of United again, doesn't it?) but they were really cannon fodder and everyone was talking about how many the Oranje would score even before van Nistelrooy came on to nail down the coffin yet further.

And the other big story that had just broken was the doping scandal surrounding Edgar Davids. The sample he gave after the Juventus-Udinese match on 4 March had come back positive for nandrolone, and the results of the second test were awaited. Davids denied any illegality the day before the Cyprus game, but he wasn't in the team that took the field in Eindhoven. Thanks to Davids and van Nistelrooy, it all looked set up for a spicy and entertaining 90 minutes - unless you'd just arrived from Larnaca.

I'd just arrived from England, and I didn't have a ticket, which was threatening to spoil not just the 90 minutes but the entire day.

The only Dutch person I'd contacted about the game was called Frank, who turned out to run a large PSV Eindhoven website. At first, he told me there was no way the stadium would sell out against Cyprus - I'd be able to just pitch up and buy a ticket at the gate. As that was exactly what I'd done for the Belgium-San Marino game in Brussels two months earlier, this sounded plausible to me, but then Frank contacted me again to say that tickets were selling faster than tulips on Mother's Day. I'd need a ticket in advance, said Frank, and for this my only option was to join the national Orange Supporters' Club. That sounded like a tough one, given that I was English to begin with, a potentially insuperable drawback; and by now the game was in just five days' time.

YOU COME WITH ME - I GET TICKETS

So instead I gave the Dutch FA a ring just to see if I could get one from them. Despite the reputation of English fans, I was an obvious neutral and, you never knew, they might therefore trust me not to cause any trouble at the game. But I was out of luck: they told me that every ticket for the game had been sold by now.

I pointed all this out to Frank, and asked him if he knew anyone who might have what are euphemistically known as 'spare' tickets, or where I might get one on the day of the game. The Markt (Market Square) in the centre of town, or a street leading off it called Stratumseind, which comprised a quarter of a mile of wall-to-wall bars, were the best places, he said. Trade would shift to the stadium area an hour or so before the game. If I called the touts' bluff and waited until just after kick-off, I'd get a ticket at less than face value. So I was in with a chance.

Eindhoven is arguably the flattest, most mind-numbingly bland and featureless city anywhere outside Milton Keynes or the US Mid-West. I'd never before seen such a bog-standard array of apartment blocks, office blocks and banks with those impersonal, dark blue shiny windows you can't see through from the outside. The editors of the biggest guidebook to Holland I could find said something on page 643 about shopping and a second-rate art gallery somewhere in the city and, well, that was it for Eindhoven as far as they were concerned. You went there on business or not at all.

Even the football club is inextricably linked to modern corporate affairs. The 'P' had been put into 'PSV Eindhoven' by electronics giant Philips, the largest single business in the city and not merely the football club's long-standing owner and sponsor, but its founder as well, back in 1913. This makes PSV a works team, albeit one that, thanks to Monday's activity in the van Nistelrooy transfer market, was about to become 19 million pounds richer.

PSV's stadium is, inevitably enough, called the Philips Stadium. England lost to Portugal here during Euro 2000, which spoilt my birthday that year. The place holds 31,000 or so, all seated. And they're mostly all suited as well. Provision for executive boxes and corporate hospitality was not merely an afterthought when the stadium was refurbished in 1988, it underpinned the whole venture. Commercialism is everywhere. Under the Oosttribune stand at one end is a branch of Toys R Us. Toys R Us sell good stuff for kids, but somehow, seeing one of their shops right there just didn't conjure up that pulse-racing, matchday, raw footballing emotion. Imagine a McDonalds under the Kop, or a megastore at Old Trafford. It would just be ridiculous.

PSV, who won the European Cup in 1988 and who qualify for the Champions League group stages just about every year, feel they're outstripping the rest of the Dutch top division and make periodic noises about linking up in a so-called Atlantic League with the leading clubs from countries like Belgium, Norway, Portugal and Scotland, who also see themselves getting squeezed out of the action at the very top of the European tree because their domestic competition doesn't stretch them enough. This might make perfect footballing sense for them, but naturally doesn't go down too well with the Dutch clubs who would be left behind.

Two hours before kick-off, I started my search for a ticket at one of the open air bars in the centre of the Markt, but if there were any touts there, they were extremely well disguised. So I finished my drink and tried my luck in a small Surinamese-run burger place on one edge of the square. All 30 or so customers inside were kitted out in orange from head to waist at least, although jeans of a more standard colour appeared to be tolerated. In the crush to be served at the counter, I asked if anyone had a ticket.

'You have no ticket? Pfffhh!' said one bloke with a wave of his hand. I took this to be an idiomatic way of saying that I'd had my chips (As it happened, I hadn't had the chance to order any yet). A lad at the first table heard me ask and passed the question on down the whole row, but there was no take-up. At least, I think he was asking on my behalf. For all I knew, he could have been saying, 'this English prat's come all the way here on an off chance, let's all have a good laugh at his expense, he'll never get in.' I gave up for the moment and concentrated on eating my burger at a stand-up counter along one side.

Two minutes later my chum from the counter appeared at my elbow. He waved a ticket under my nose.

YOU COME WITH ME - I GET TICKETS

'Do you still want a ticket?' he asked.

Through a mouthful of chips I said that I did.

'What would you give me for this one?' he asked. The face value was 75 Guilders, or a little over £20.

I thought quickly. 'I'll give you 100,' I offered.

He thought about it. 'No,' he said after a second or two. '100 is too much. Ha! I think I will go to the game myself! You can get one at the stadium for 85.' With which he walked out the door and disappeared, leaving me wondering what he was on, and whether it was legal. In Holland, it probably was.

As the last chip went down, I figured that ticket trade could hardly be any less brisk at the stadium. When I got there, I found the orange-clad hordes massing, and all of them were going straight in, as they all had tickets. I'd forgotten how second-class you feel when you're the only one that doesn't have a ticket for the big event. I felt I should keep a bit of an eye out for the police, but although they were there, it was all very low key. Cyprus, after all, were unlikely to have that many fans with them and the potential for trouble was virtually nil. I'd been there in Poland the previous October when fans of local rivals Widzew and LKS had had a go at each other, but tonight's Dutch fans couldn't even do that, as PSV don't have any serious cross-town rivals. But what local law enforcement would make of ticket touting, I wasn't sure.

The corner was the best place, said one or two people I asked. But no one was playing. There just weren't any touts. I just missed a sale as a bloke with a few in his back pocket sold his last just as I worked out what he was doing, and that appeared to be it. For a while I teamed up with an English journalist, obviously on the van Nistelrooy trail, who was also ticketless. Time was getting on and it looked more and more as if neither of us was going to be getting in. I was hacked off enough for it to strike me that practically everything Frank had told me had turned out to be wide of the mark: there were no tickets available on the night, there were no touts in the marketplace, and none at the stadium either. Maybe his line about prices dropping after kick-off would prove to be accurate, but for that to happen, some touts would first of all have to show up.

YOU HAVE NO TICKET? PFFFHH!

With under half an hour to go I saw a group of four or five people gather round handing out tickets among themselves. I went up and asked if they had one over. Yes, they said, they did. They'd come from Amsterdam and at the last minute, their friend couldn't come. Did that mean I could have it, I asked. Sure, no problem, they said. Except, Wim's got the ticket and he's gone off that way, hoping to sell it.

We scoured the place for Wim. Or at least, one of them nonchalantly wandered off to find him. After an anxious (for me) minute or two, Wim was located and brought back, and the ticket was mine - at face value, which helped buy the resulting round of beers. My new friends were all Dutch apart from Jane, an Irish girl living in Amsterdam.

'You should have been there in September,' she said, 'when Ireland played in Holland. The game finished 2-2, and Ireland should really have won, but they let slip a two-goal lead. The game was in the Amsterdam ArenA. A great day. But there were 10,000 empty seats.'

I was only slightly thrown when she then admitted she hadn't actually been at the game herself. 'They said it would be full, so I didn't try to get in.' Tonight, she had a tiny radio with her, which she used to check the progress of Mick McCarthy's team against potential Andorran giantkillers. In the end Ireland won that game 3-1, but Andorra scored first, fortunately when Jane wasn't listening.

Inside the stadium, the home team's mascot, Dutchy (ho ho) the Lion, was parading around in the penalty area at our end wearing an orange number seven shirt. I don't know if these furry animals are intended to inspire loyalty or affection, but at least Dutchy didn't look quite as manky as the kangaroo suit I'd seen being worn by the Bohemians Prague mascot. The Bohemians Prague kangaroo fixation dates all the way back to a club tour to Australia in 1926, and now before their home games one of the club's minor officials puts the suit on, waddles inelegantly out to the centre circle and waves a bit. Once the game's underway, he hangs out behind the main stand where he waits till half time. I was round the back of the stand looking for a beer when I saw him unzip his own head for a pre-interval fag-break. On my way back to the terrace I saw that one of that day's Bohemians' substitutes had joined him for a quick and probably non-contractual drag.

On every seat in the Philips Stadium tonight was a free match programme, ironically with a pre-doping scandal picture of Edgar Davids on the cover, and an inflatable plastic crown, which as chance would have it was also orange and came in its own little plastic bag, complete with a vinyl puncture patch repair kit, this being a tidy country like Holland. Luckily, the seats were so steeply banked that everyone could happily wear a big orange plastic crown on their head not only without embarrassment but also without blocking the view in the row behind. So everyone duly inflated their crown and wore it, apart from the suits in the main stand, although they did join in the Mexican waves. The result, seen from the other side of the stadium, was a wall of orange from the front row to the back, as good a way of emphasising home advantage as you could want. The South Koreans did the same thing, only in red and even better, at the finals a year later.

What really impressed me about Dutch football spectators, at least the ones in the stadium tonight, was the way the game is followed by both sexes and all ages but hasn't lost the passionate nature of its following. Big games are definitely a family occasion in places like Finland and Iceland, and it's great that children there can watch safely and with a good view, but there's somehow something over-sanitised and anaemic about it all in those countries. Here, multi-generational families wrapped up in Hup Holland! shrouds were chatting to and rubbing shoulders with distinctly alternative-looking types whose personal grooming was not out of the very top drawer, who had dodgy bright orange (orange. Come on, I thought you folks wanted to be different) haircuts, and who smoked the unforgettably-named 'Halfzwaare Shag' roll-your-own tobacco. Yet neither group had the slightest problem with the other. Everyone could make the game and the occasion what they wanted it to be, and that was fine with everyone else. A very high proportion of the European Championship-winning Dutch team of 1988 was of Surinamese descent, a point not lost on one of its leading lights, Ruud Gullit, who said at the time that Holland was a liberal and tolerant country. Well, here tonight was another encouraging example of where tolerance in society can lead.

The atmosphere was noisy but (until half-time) not overly reliant on hype through the PA. Four giant screens were in operation, as I guess you'd expect in the Philips Stadium, and up went the names of the players. Sadly not one of the Cypriot names meant anything to me, but nearly all of the Dutch side were household names in the UK, including Hasselbaink (Followers of Chelsea please note, that's Jerrel Hasselbaink. Any of you know where the Jimmy Floyd thing came from?). All the others were there. Apart from that naughty boy Davids, that is. Van der Sar, Cocu, Kluivert, Overmars, Seedorf, Zenden, Frank de Boer, the boy Nistelrooy warming the bench… quite a team.

But after half an hour it was still 0-0 and the locals weren't happy. Then Hasselbaink, from a free-kick, and Overmars, from open play, put Holland two up. Meanwhile Kluivert went through his full repertoire of tricks; backheels, side flicks, bicycle kicks, you name it, and then finished up by scoring a goal in the last minute before half-time.

A 3-0 lead was excuse enough for the man on the PA to crank up the volume. The medley of tunes that followed included You'll Never Walk Alone, the perenially fresh-sounding Here We Go, Queen's We Are the Champions and, bizarrely, the Hokey-Cokey, segueing seamlessly into, as you would expect, Verdi's Chorus of the Hebrew Slaves.

Holland lost their way again in the second half, as if the players were also waiting for the moment you felt the whole crowd had come to see - the introduction of van Nistelrooy, after 71 minutes, on his return to international competition. Various Cypriot players and subs had been politely applauded on and off, but van Nistelrooy raised the roof. His rasping 25-yard strike for his side's final goal eleven minutes later had 'I'm back' written all over it and made the net bulge in all the right places. Maybe Holland should have beaten this opposition by more, but seeing the man of the moment score on his comeback made everyone happy - unless you'd just arrived from Larnaca. But it didn't look as if anyone had. Two people just below me, who were forlornly waving the flag of Holland's Group Two rivals Portugal, looked like the only fans Cyprus had tonight.

So now it was no wins in 8 attempts for the Cypriots against the Dutch. They'd been hammered 8-0 in 1988, but we know how good that Holland side was.

We may know better now, but that night it seemed inconceivable that Holland would not qualify for the finals the following year. In the manner of coaches and captains everywhere, however, Louis van Gaal and Frank de Boer put on a front of not being too pleased with their side's easy win tonight. 'We wasted lots of chances, it could have been a lot better, we played really badly, Seedorf played a weak game, the first half was moderate and after half-time it was even worse, we resorted to the long ball too easily, it only got going in the second half once I brought van Nistelrooy on, we played too hastily, and we lost the ball too much,' said the pair of them about their team's thumping 4-0 win, which gave them the best goal difference in what was always going to be a tough group. As Basil Fawlty once said, 'otherwise OK?'.

10.

Endrew, Frankly Speaking, Are You Eriksson Fen?

Russia - Yugoslavia, Luzhniki Stadium, Moscow, Saturday 2 June 2001

THEY SAY THE BEST kind of dog is a hot dog, if only because you can rely on it to feed the hand that bites it, rather than the other way round. I wanted my next half-time hot dog to come from somewhere dodgier than the last one - dodgier geographically that is, as opposed to anatomically. The game in Eindhoven had been enjoyable, and had featured the best goals and the liveliest crowd I'd seen so far, but other than that the whole thing was just too normal. Dutch people are just like us, only more relaxed, more tolerant and a lot better at foreign languages. Holland against Cyprus wasn't really a clash of footballing titans, and the countries had no underlying political scores to settle through the football. Being ticketless 20 minutes before kick-off, having to do something about it, and still finding time for a pre-match beer inside the stadium with Wim and his mates had been about as non-standard as it got.

But a clash of Slav giants in post-communist Moscow looked a bit more like it. Yugoslavia were getting to grips with the qualifying campaign now. They'd built up a bit of a fixture backlog in autumn 2000, when they couldn't play any of their games as the country faced more important business, namely ending the career of the lad Milosevic - Slobodan, that is, not Savo, Villa fans may be sad to hear. Russia were clear leaders of their qualifying group at this point, and Slovenia, Switzerland and Yugoslavia were slugging it out for second. The Swiss campaign had been anonymous so far, and Slovenia were picking up a lot of drawn games, including against the Faroes, which had cost them two points they might find it hard to make up, as Scotland were to discover the following year in their Euro 2004 opener. This all left Yugoslavia with a decent chance.

For this game, instead of turning up at the stadium with no ticket, which I pretty much knew I could get away with in Holland, I had four tickets as good as in my pocket before leaving England, as both of my friend's Russian contacts had come up with two. Although there were 76,000 empty yellow plastic seats in the 86,000-seater Luzhniki Stadium in March for Russia's home game against the Faroes (do you remember the islanders' bobble-hatted 'keeper the day they beat Austria a few years back? He said his mum told him to wear it), Yugoslavia was potentially much more of a bums-on-seats affair for the average Muscovite than bobble-hatted 'keepers.

Moscow is a long way from anywhere, and times are hard in Belgrade, but I still thought there'd be a few Serbs making the trip, as this was as important a game as Yugoslavia faced in their group. I was wrong. According to one of Red Star Belgrade's 'Delije Srbija' group of hardcore fans, none of their group would be going, because they were in an ongoing dispute with the Yugoslav FA and the new, post-Milosevic regime in Belgrade over the name of the national side. They wanted it to be called Serbia, and not Yugoslavia, they wanted a different anthem, they wanted this, they wanted that, they all blamed the new Government (despite having just helped install it thanks to their part in overthrowing the old Government) and they were all going to sit in Belgrade until they got what they wanted. In early 2003, they eventually did, at least over the anthem, and later the name.

These people were used to getting what they wanted. In autumn 2000, Red Star fans ('Delije' means 'Warriors') had been at the forefront of the 'Milosevic out' campaign, chanting anti-regime slogans from the north end of their ground and then, on 5 October 2000, spearheading that day's march on the Belgrade Parliament building. Milosevic's militia attacked them, but the Parliament was stormed by the protesters, and from that day on the writing was on the wall for the Milosevic old guard.

Having that direct a role in the overthrow of Milosevic appeared to be some sort of a turnaround for a club that, in the early 1990s, had numbered the paramilitary thug Arkan in its ranks. Arkan's real name was Zeljko Raznatovic (so it's easy to see why he was better known as Arkan), and he was Milosevic's dirty deeds man, at least while Milosevic found the arrangement an expedient one. In his spare time, Arkan was the unifier of the various Red Star fan groups, and led them, under the name Delije Srbija, from the late 1980s until about 1992 when he moved on to other things - such as taking control of Belgrade's black economy.

But Arkan couldn't leave football behind. In 1996 he bought a club of his own, Obilic, then languishing in the lower Serbian leagues. By intimidating referees and opposition strikers alike, he and his thugs helped Obilic make it into the top flight. They finished fourth in the 2001-02 season - enough for an Intertoto Cup place. However, Arkan himself didn't live to see Obilic's brief European campaign. He reaped what he had sown on 15 January 2000, when four gunmen with high-calibre weapons shot him at point blank range in the lobby of the Belgrade Intercontinental Hotel. Some have alleged that Milosevic, desperate to cling to power, was behind the killing.

The Intercontinental continued to use the sofa he'd been sitting on, but it did take a while to reupholster it nicely and get all the blood out of the cushions.

As we were engaged in an e-mail exchange and he couldn't plant one on me for saying it, I pointed out to the stayaway Red Star fan that when Russia had played Yugoslavia in Belgrade in April 2001 (and won 1-0), it was a 40,000 sell-out. So what was his problem about watching the national side? Back came a loud, disapproving electronic harrumph from the Red Star webman. Those misguided 40,000 fans may have gone along, but that didn't signify those fans' approval of anything he personally was against. Or something like that. It was simply that there was no other national team to support, he said, so all 40,000 had feebly yielded to the temptation of watching what was clearly the biggest game in Belgrade for years. He said that Partizan Belgrade fans were apparently more ready to support a 'Yugoslavia' team than their rivals at Red Star, so it must have been them that had gone along.

But that was the home game. Whatever the reasons, if the fanatics weren't travelling to Moscow, it was unlikely the more fairweather ones would. So no Yugoslavs in Moscow then.

I'd been to Russia before, so I knew a little of what to expect. Mafia intimidation at Sheremetevo airport means that although you can get an ordinary bus into the city, you have to get on board behind a disused hangar somewhere two miles away out by Runway G, which usually turns out to be blocked off because the JCBs have just moved in to repair it. Russians have a number of things that they Like Doing Best, and closing everything in sight so that they can repair it comes pretty near the top of the list. Russians are a studious lot, and so attending academic symposiums comes next. But mending things is a clear winner - which could explain why everything is so shoddily built to begin with. That way they get the evident pleasure much earlier of closing it down for weeks while they fix it.

The apparent non-availablity of buses is designed to drive you into the hands of the taxi sharks, unless you have a pre-arranged transfer deal with your hotel. But compared to Romania, the taxi touts at Sheremetevo are pussy cats. Instead of having eight of them surround me all the way down the exit road, this lot took no for an answer first time and left me in peace to catch the bus.

Everything about Russia is twice the normal size, making you feel as if the view through a magnifying glass is the new reality. Blocks of flats house thousands at a time. Metro stations are twice the distance apart as in London or Paris, and the trains run at twice the depth - and twice as often. Road traffic averaged 60mph outside my hotel window, and some traffic lights will stay green for nearly five minutes at a time.

With hotels, too, the Russians clearly feel that size does matter. Don't expect to find a small, family-run establishment anywhere in

ARE YOU ERIKSSON FEN?

Moscow. Instead, be prepared for enormous empty restaurants, 40-storey buildings, a hall for attending symposiums in, 16 lifts, half of them closed for repair, and a 'service bureau' (or 'ugly interfering old bat', depending on what sort of day you've had) on each floor. If that's your idea of perfect away-from-home accommodation, then Moscow is the place for you. The love affair with size carries over to the bill too: you can pay over $300 per night for a room in the city if you want, never mind that that's 3 months' earnings for the average Muscovite.

The evening I arrived, the phone rang in my room at about 11pm. It was Anatoly, about the tickets he'd got for us. I knew already that he wasn't really a football fan and that there was an international symposium in town that weekend which would probably rule him out of the football anyway, but I still wanted the tickets, because I could pass them on to friends of Ilya's. Ilya's mother had got hold of the other two tickets. If Ilya and I had those, I guessed Ilya would be able to whistle up a couple of his mates at short notice to come along on Anatoly's tickets. Anatoly said that his wife would call in at the hotel on her way over to another symposium, presumably a different one to Anatoly's.

With four tickets safely in the bag, I headed off into the city. Lenin is still dead, and still in his marble mausoleum on Red Square, despite the plans of some in the Russian Government to remove him for good. You aren't allowed in with a camera - the militia on duty will find it on you and turf you out the queue. Once you're past them, you go in, down a steep staircase to the left, and into the subterranean hall where Lenin lies. The guards down there physically push you to keep moving if you stop even for a few seconds, and a minute is the most you can make it take to shuffle round the three sides of the glass case.

Right alongside Red Square, but twice the distance from the mausoleum that you think it's going to be, is a three-storey underground shopping centre, a project of the populist and, for many, genuinely popular mayor of Moscow, Yuri Luzhkov. He has changed the Moscow skyline more than anyone since Stalin himself. The city has been adorned (or desecrated) by his massive projects, of which the undergound mall is at least tucked away out of sight.

YOU COME WITH ME - I GET TICKETS

It was getting on for kick-off time. The metro train was jammed with fans, many of whom made their Polish counterparts look tame. As in Poland, all of them were young men. Hair of ordinary, or indeed any, length was not an option for these guys. One lad near me had the word 'ROSSIYA' - 'Russia' - tattooed in blue onto his shaven skull. After Russia lost to arch-rivals Japan in the 2002 finals, fans like him showed what they could do, by rioting across much of the city centre, killing two people, injuring 100 and terrorising Japanese visitors to the city. Sixty of the thugs were arrested. The only two instances of World Cup-related hooliganism that I came across - this riot in Moscow, and the Widzew-LKS fight in Lodz the previous October - were both the work of East European skinheads.

I'd arranged to meet Ilya and his friends, Andrey and Aleksandr, on the platform at Frunzenskaya, the metro stop before Sportivnaya. Like Wembley Park underground station in London, Sportivnaya metro station is not just the only practical way to get to the national stadium, it's also a good half mile away from it. The entrance hall of the metro station was packed with police, militia and uniformed Interior Ministry troops. As we came out at street level it was obvious which way we should go, which was just as well. Somehow these policemen didn't look like they would be too inclined to put a paternal arm around your shoulder and give you directions, should you feel a little lost; never mind going along the way with you on their bicycle, telling you to mind how you go and tipping their helmet as they said goodbye.

Ilya, Andrey and Aleksandr were students of 'World Economics' at Moscow State University. Their hair was almost a centimetre long in places, which made them look like Seventies rock stars in comparison to those around us. Aleksandr's English wasn't quite up to the standard of his friends', but Andrey and Ilya both spoke the language very well, almost too correctly at times, apart from the way they called me Endrew rather than Andrew. Andrey, who looked alarmingly like former England rugby captain Phil de Glanville, wanted to know all about me.

ARE YOU ERIKSSON FEN?

'Endrew, in England, do you have a wife? What is your occupation? And, er, frankly speaking, what is your opinion of defence of English team? Are you Eriksson fen? And, er, in which month is your birthday?' he asked. It was all leading up to the crunch question: 'What is your opinion of Moscow?'

I told him that Moscow was a lot more fun to be in than the last time I'd been here, without letting on how long ago that was; that my birthday was in a few days' time, in the middle of June, and that I was watching top international football matches across Europe, preferably meeting the locals in various bars before and afterwards to drink plenty of the country in question's finest beer. (Apparently irony-free, an Austrian friend of mine later described this activity as a 'European Ethnology' tour, which was quite generous of her, all in all.)

Then Andrey asked if I could help him get a job in the UK, announcing as he did so that we were twins. With mental alarm bells beginning to ring ever so slightly, I asked him what he meant. We might share versions of the same name, but I didn't feel I looked that much like Phil de Glanville. 'You know, Twins,' he said. 'The Zodiac sign. My birthday is in the middle of June, too.'

By now we had come out from an underpass and were approaching the Luzhniki stadium. It had been the athletics venue for the 1980 Moscow Olympics, which took place just after the Soviet invasion of Afghanistan and were therefore boycotted by many Western nations, including the UK and the US. Now the UK and the US have invaded Afghanistan themselves, and the Russians are cock-a-hoop about it.

Recently, Mayor Luzhkov had bought the stadium, as people like him do, and made it the home ground for his team, Torpedo Moscow, in a ground-share deal with Spartak. You couldn't help feeling that Torpedo's games must lack a little for atmosphere, being played in an 86,000-seater stadium in front of four-figure crowds. The place looked as if it hadn't been used for athletics at all since 1980. So gleaming for the Olympics, it's now muddy and ramshackle, and if it rains there are big pools of water on the running track. It was a wonder Mayor Luzhkov hadn't yet closed it down to repair it.

YOU COME WITH ME - I GET TICKETS

Everywhere there were stalls selling Torpedo Moscow souvenirs alongside Russian national team ones, including those velvety pointy hats in bright colours you now see at football matches just about everywhere. Andrey and Ilya left me in no doubt about just how naff they considered these hats to be. After an authentically Russian Pepsi, we looked around for the way in. There was mean-looking, heavy duty security everywhere, shielded, helmeted, you name it. And that was just the horses. Without a single Yugoslav (sorry, Serbian) in sight, you had to wonder why they bothered. I asked Andrey what it was all about.

'It is because of Spartak Moscow fans,' he said. 'They make many problems, they are very aggressive.' Unfortunately, this may well be true: I'd seen pictures in a Russian monthly football magazine of a large-scale terraces dust-up only a few weeks before involving Spartak and CSKA fans, although there was no word on who started it. 'What Do The Fans Want?' asked the headline plaintively.

'So what are you then,' I asked Andrey, 'a Dinamo fan? Torpedo?' Despite the lack of hair, he looked like one of the least aggressive people you could wish to meet.

'No,' he said, 'I am a Spartak fan. But I do not think there will be problems today.'

Besides the police, there was a large army presence, and units both of Interior Ministry troops and OMON riot control, not to mention spotters in the stands wearing plain clothes and bright yellow armbands, which made the plain clothes a tad pointless. Just to be on the safe side, alcohol was banned, all spectators were bodily searched four times, and X-rayed, airport-style, once. Then they were allowed in. I thought they were after cameras, so I wrapped mine up in the jacket I was carrying and just held it in my hand. No one found it. And yet - there was no crowd trouble, so the authorities could point to a successful operation, unlike their Polish counterparts in Lodz, where rival local fans had enthusiastically gone for each other, and the police, with any missiles that lay to hand. And the riot after the Japan game in the finals took the Russian authorities by surprise: surely no one could riot at midday in the city centre after watching a game on TV, could they? As it turned out, Russian fans could.

ARE YOU ERIKSSON FEN?

The day after the game I met up with Oleg, who ran one of the main Spartak websites. As a Spartak fan, he thought his club's reputation for hooliganism was unfair, but then admitted to a long list of incidents caused by Spartakisti. For him this justified a police presence that we in the West would regard as heavy-handed - unless English fans were involved, that is.

On each seat in the main stadium was a piece of card in one of the three colours of the Russian flag. On the back of it were the words of what Ilya called the 'national hymn'. When the teams came out the idea was to hold the card up, so that the crowd formed a giant Russian flag and terrified the opposition by being word-perfect with the national hymn.

Propaganda freebies of some sort or another had become standard at any game where there was a chance of a five-figure crowd. I still had my Dutch inflatable orange plastic crown, and of course the repair patch that came with it. Later on, the Croats and the Ukrainians, presumably on a smaller budget, had to be a bit less generous. The Croats supplied what amounted to plastic laundry bags you had to put your hands inside and hold up - cunningly reading the words of the national hymn off the back as you did so. The plastic theme was picked up by the marketing agency employed by the Ukrainian federation, who came up with the brilliant idea of giving everyone a giant upside-down bin liner to wear, poncho-style. The upper tier wore blue, and all 41,000 people in the lower tier of the stand got a yellow one. It looked as if corruption had struck the Tour de France again and arguments about who should have the leader's jersey had got seriously out of hand.

The game kicked off and Russia were probably a bit lucky to go ahead after 25 minutes with a long range speculative shot from Spartak Moscow's Yuri Kovtun. Just seven minutes later the Yugoslavs equalised with a much better goal - a pinpoint cross for Predrag Mijatovic to head downwards. Nigmatullin in the Russian goal got down well and grasped the ball - but it had crossed the line, albeit only just. I was directly in line with it and I can confirm that the linesman got it right. What is it about Russians, linesmen, and whether the ball crosses the line?

YOU COME WITH ME - I GET TICKETS

Mayor Luzhkov was at the game as well. In fact, he got the biggest cheer of the night so far when his presence was announced, 24 minutes into the game. Unfortunately for him he was upstaged a minute later when Russia got their goal and 75,980 people raised the stadium roof. The other 20 people there turned out to be Yugoslavs after all. Mostly in family groups and probably resident in Moscow anyway, they happened to be in the row directly behind me and Ilya. At half-time, they obviously weren't comfortable with a 1-1. 'It is a game we have to win,' one of them said to me. 'If we only draw today, we already will have very little chance.' I felt that that was being a bit too pessimistic too early. Yugoslavia only started to have very little chance after carelessly throwing away a lead in Belgrade later in the year against Slovenia, their main rivals for the play-off spot.

While the World Cup finals were on in the Far East, I contacted Delije Srbija again, to get a view from them on their country's footballing decline, which probably dates back to the time when they went out unluckily at the quarter-final stage at Italia '90 (to Argentina on penalties, a World Cup exit route which has a certain familiar ring to it). I was expecting to be told that exclusion from Euro '92, the breakup of the old Yugoslavia, a decade of economic corruption, and brutal civil wars leading to three months' bombing by NATO might have had something to do with the country's footballing misfortunes. Instead, the fans I heard back from placed the blame fairly and squarely at the feet of the country's FA.

'It is a nice little scam they have going,' Marko told me. 'They invite players whose club contract is nearly up to play for the national team in order to increase their value. In return those players give the FA officials a percentage of their new club contract.' This results, he said, in aged has-beens playing without real commitment, and often out of position, at the expense of hungrier, more talented players at the start of their careers. Taking teams for Serbia's summer 2002 friendlies as a guide, he pointed out that, of the likely Yugoslavian starting eleven to play Italy in the opening Euro 2004 qualifier, only two were under 25, and seven were 29 or older. And just fancy that, he said, many of those seven (like Mihajlovic, 33, Mirkovic, 32, Jokanovic, 34, and

Mijatovic, 33) would then be in the final year of their club contract. These players would surely be too long in the tooth to build a team around for the Euro 2004 finals. Croatia could point to third place at France '98, achieved with an ageing squad, but this Yugoslavian outfit would be older still. At the time, Sinisa Mihajlovic had played fewer than 10 games for Lazio, yet he was regularly in the national starting eleven.

Back in Moscow, it was half-time and the big screen was giving us latest scores from the other games played today. This made for better viewing than the real game in front of us, which in the second half was foot-shufflingly dull. Both sides were sitting back, apparently happy with what they had.

With 20 minutes to go, the PA announcements began. About every three minutes between then and the final whistle, a pre-recorded voice encouraged us to 'observe orderliness and calm' on the way out. Just to be sure, they kept us back for an hour at the end as they very slowly emptied the stadium, block by block. Entertainment, up to a point, came from big screen cartoons, Bugs Bunny-style but without the sophistication the name implies, and interrupted repeatedly by a bizarre advertisement called 'Athlete Armageddon', in which an animated version of Dutch international Edgar Davids 'takes on a 40-ton truck' and proceeds to rip it to bits with his bare hands. This was in the very week in which the real life Davids was banned for performance-enhancing drug usage.

Ours was one of the last blocks to be let out, and so there was ample opportunity to reflect on how soulless these big stadiums get when they're empty. Andrey and Aleksandr were waiting for us by the steps to our sector, and we started walking back towards the metro. It was well after ten o'clock, and still broad daylight. Andrey said he wasn't really that much of a fan and that the second half had been terrible. Still, at least he was there, eh? On the way out he spotted that one of the bored-looking soldiers standing in a long crowd-control line on the concourse was not only having a discreet and militarily unsanctioned fag, but also was his mate from school back in Ryazan, so we hung around a bit while Andrey caught up with the latest goss about gourmet army cuisine and the ritual bullying of this year's conscripts - of which his friend could well have been one.

To be fair, you couldn't blame the Russians for taking stadium security very seriously. Few people in the West know that in 1982, this same stadium was the scene of a crowd disaster that dwarfed even Hillsborough - something like 340 people were crushed to death, three and a half times the Hillsborough figure, and of course in the dying Leonid Brezhnev's Soviet Union, this kind of thing wasn't meant to happen, so it was all covered up, and stayed covered up for years. Today's heavy-handed approach was in force all the way back to Sportivnaya metro: everyone shuffled obediently along a humanly-formed 20-yard wide avenue made by soldiers standing shoulder to shoulder along both sides. For all the efficiency of the Moscow metro, with trains every two minutes most of the day, 76,000 people suddenly reliant on its services stretches even its capacity, and the stadium was almost certainly being evacuated according to how quickly the metro could clear the platforms.

'This is my limo,' said Ilya, as we walked back to his Soviet-era Fiat-lookalike effort, having gone one stop on the metro. The four of us had agreed something to eat would be a good idea, and as luck would have it, his street atlas was sponsored by McDonalds. The 20 or so main landmarks of the city were clearly marked. And if you looked really carefully, you could see where Red Square and the Kremlin were as well, and not just the 20 or so McDonalds.

There wasn't quite the need for Ilya to drive there at 80 mph, which is what he did, but it meant we got to one of Ronald McDonald's restaurants about two minutes quicker, so I guess it was probably worth the danger. The Beach Boys were playing as people ate their burgers. We were now in the Arbat area of the city, which is to Moscow what Notting Hill is to London or the Left Bank to Paris - posh, arty and full of students and foreigners who can recognise quality when they see it. McDonalds was packed.

By now it was nearly midnight. We said goodbye to Andrey, but for Ilya and Aleksandr, midnight on Saturday was clearly the perfect time to pay their respects at Victory Park, the latest outsize memorial to World War II, or the Great Patriotic War, as it is more correctly known in these parts. Over 20 million Soviet citizens died in the conflict and the memory is actively kept alive to this day. The Soviet victory over Hitler's Germany was the one really unarguable achievement of the Communist regime, and if in later Soviet days you felt the memory was being kept alive a little artificially, perhaps to focus attention away from the shortages and repressions of the 1970s and 80s, you would now have to concede that, even ten or more years after the USSR broke up, the War has lost nothing of its grip on the imagination of the former Soviet Union. The park was lit in red - one fountain of blood-red water for each day of the war, which in the USSR's case was around 1,400 days: that makes for a lot of fountains and a big electricity bill. Mayor Luzhkov had got in on the act here as well, commissioning another of his huge monuments, but this one was welcomed as being in touch with the public mood. It was striking to see how many young people - like Ilya himself, who was 19 - and families with children were here, even at so late an hour. Parked a little way off were some WWII-era Soviet tanks, which Ilya showed me, proudly explaining that his grandfather had himself been a 'tankist', although, having been born in 1933 (generations are short in Russia), grandad had been too young to fight in WWII. The Russians visit war memorials on Saturday nights. In the UK, we watch 'Who Wants to be a Millionaire?'

But then maybe we're better drivers. We set off again, this time in search of my hotel, at the now expected breakneck speed and in the now expected wrong direction. After a mega-detour taking in the south-eastern suburbs, the north-western suburbs and the world's biggest railway marshalling yard, Ilya stopped for petrol.

'My car eats a lot,' he explained, pointing at the petrol tank. 'Only 100km for 15 litres!' He suddenly remembered that I was an imperialist. 'I don't know how many pints per mile!'

It worked out at something well under 20mpg, which would put his car firmly in the ravenous bracket. Off we went, at 60mph in third gear, a driving style which may have had a slight bearing on the fuel consumption. I was still in the back seat, but over the not inconsiderable engine noise I could just about hear him yelling some excuse about 'not having time to tune it'. For all that, the lift back to my hotel was very welcome, as by the time we'd worked out where we were all the buses had stopped for the night. They dropped me off at around quarter to two. Rod Stewart was playing in the lift on the way up to my room. I preferred the Beach Boys, all in all.

11.

Looks Like He's Putting Up One Of The Nets

Iceland - Bulgaria, Laugardalsvollur Stadium, Reykjavik, Wednesday 6 June 2001

THE ROOM FACED NORTH, so of course it got the sun all the time. All night anyway. A lot of visitors to Iceland from the lands of darkness to the south are so disorientated by having the sun streaming into their rooms at 2am that the locals have started to build hotel rooms with windows facing back into the corridor instead of to the north. For me, having travelled half the night already, not much was going to keep me awake.

Given the country's tiny population (about the same as Coventry) and their climate, Icelandic football does amazingly well. The Bulgarians, today's opposition, were probably too savvy to be thinking that this game represented an easy three points. A disproportionately high number of Icelandic players are attached to English clubs - leading Premiership sides at that, not just teams like Stoke. Iceland had recently lost only narrowly to France, they were to put three goals past the Czech Republic in September 2001, and they came within an ace of automatic qualification for Euro 2004 ahead of Germany, so pushovers they weren't, and aren't.

Iceland's on-field achievements have come against con-siderable odds. It's pretty cold up there, so the domestic season has to be packed into many fewer months than in other countries. Playing home World Cup games in October, as they sometimes have to do, is really stretching things. Another footballing problem other countries don't have is the ferocious and near-constant wind. However many layers of clothes you wear, it's always one too few. Wind of that intensity for so long makes it difficult for anything more complex than moss to grow, so the next challenge is finding enough flat grass for a pitch, especially as UEFA regulations do give preference to grassy areas that don't suddenly develop geothermal hot springs in the goalmouth or the centre circle. There are stories of law-abiding Icelandic folk being disturbed in the course of a quiet night at home in front of the telly by gallons of boiling water suddenly shooting up from under the carpet. That's not a scene from Poltergeist 3, that's for real. Another house had its roof demolished by a tree falling into it. A common enough occurrence, you might think, but only in Iceland does it happen because its roots have been killed off by the boiling water of a new hot spot. You half expect to see all the country's footballers wearing heat-resistant boots. Maybe this is where their team's nimble footwork comes from - with things liable to get a tad warm underfoot at any moment, you get used to hopping around a bit.

All this free hot water keeps the electricity and heating bills down very nicely. In general, however, the rumour that Iceland is one of the most expensive countries in the world is completely true. Even though I didn't get into it until 3am, my 10' by 8' hotel room was still 60 quid a night. Had I been able to buy one at that time of night, I would have found that beer costs the standard Scandinavian/Arctic five pounds a pint. At least this means the police don't have to worry that much about arranging 12 o'clock kick-offs to prevent people getting too tanked up beforehand.

As if Icelanders would do such a thing anyway, whatever the price of a pint. I've never been anywhere more honest, tolerant, and crime-free. The whole country is a place where you can leave your car unlocked, your front door open, and money lying around on the table. Even your mobile won't get nicked, because everyone's got at least two already. They're just pleased that you decided to come all this way to visit their country.

Usually for games in Scandinavian countries - well, on the basis of Finland and Norway so far - I would just ring up, and a ticket for Finland-Albania, or whatever, was mine, once I'd persuaded them that I really meant it, which did occasionally take a while. For this game, for the first and what turned out to be only time, I'd persuaded a couple of English friends to come to the match with me, although that maybe had rather less to do with any thrills promised by the fixture and a lot more to do with the fact that they were going to be in Reykjavik on business anyway. So I wanted three tickets.

When I rang the Icelandic FA (just say 'Knattspyrnusamband Islands' and they'll put you through), I was connected to someone called Geir, who was on his mobile somewhere. Explaining what I wanted, we chatted a bit about the game, and about Iceland's chances of, as Geir put it, 'getting a result' at home to Malta the weekend before the Bulgaria game. If I e-mailed Geir personally with my credit card details, he said, he'd fix the tickets for me to collect on the day of the game. I discovered later that Geir was the Secretary of the Icelandic Football Association, but I can tell you he's happy to stop whatever he's doing and help you get a ticket or three. Try that in England.

Kick-off was at 6pm. After a very windy morning seeing if I could find a restaurant that didn't serve fish with everything, I prepared for the excitement of the match in the traditional local way. That meant spending a demanding couple of hours relaxing in one of the downtown hot springs, where the water is 38 or 39 degrees C - about hot shower temperature. Then I went over to the stadium to collect the tickets.

Football fever did not seem to have this city in its grip, although Bulgaria had at least turned up expecting a game. I knew that - I'd seen half the Bulgarian squad in town earlier on, engaged in some pre-match retail therapy, wearing tracksuits, all relaxed and quite happy to be photographed outside Top Shop by curious locals. But at 2.30pm the huge car park outside the stadium was deserted but for about seven distinctly chunky pick-up trucks and 4 by 4s. It looked as if no one was about. Then I saw three Sainsbury's Homebase-style wooden sheds off to one side, where they were selling tickets, or would have been, had anyone been buying. There are only two or three games of any consequence played in Iceland all year, so you had to wonder why they needed three sheds to sell tickets when one bloke equipped with something like a raffle book could probably have done the job OK.

I went from hut to hut asking if they had my tickets, but none of them did, so I wandered up and down outside the ground for a while, peering through windows and trying the odd door handle here and there, hoping to find someone who might help me get the tickets that Geir had gone to all the trouble of reserving for me. Eventually I found a two-room building that was open. The 'Knattspyrnusamband Islands' sign above the door showed that this was the Icelandic answer to Lancaster Gate. A couple of people looked up when I walked in, clearly a bit surprised to see anyone three hours before Iceland's biggest home game of 2001. I explained why I was there, and the girl behind one desk just reached out a hand, picked up an envelope with my name on it and handed it over. She was very nice about it and didn't laugh at me at all or make it plain she thought I was a saddo for coming all this way to watch Iceland play football. Geir had done his stuff. I was in.

I had three tickets for Iceland against Bulgaria. There were very few occasions when I wondered just why I was charging all over Europe watching football matches whose outcome was of no conceivable significance to me, but this was one of them.

I'd found the restaurant that served chicken rather than fish, I'd seen the quaint old painted houses in the city centre, I'd done the hot tubs, and I had an hour or so before meeting Marcus and Steve. I went back to the hotel for some food, and switched on the TV in my room. Until a few years ago, there was no Icelandic TV on Thursdays at all, nor for the whole of July, so that the TV people could get a holiday. Now, you can get UK Channel 5. Half the population of the UK still can't get it, but in this shoebox hotel room in the middle of the Atlantic, it was loud and clear, as the not altogether dulcet tones of Jonathan Pearce described the Republic of Ireland going one up, away to Estonia.

Marcus and Steve were unlikely to be feeling as relaxed, tubbed and stress-free as I was. They were insurance assessors doing their annual factory visit, and they'd spent the day wearing hard hats and flame-proof overalls near the furnaces at a huge aluminium smelting plant up the coast, 50 miles outside town, and had had to cut their meeting short and take a few major risks as read so as to get back in time for the game. Their company went bust the following year.

Marcus rang about half way through the first half of the Estonia game in Tallinn. It was nearly 4.30 and he and Steve had just arrived at the stadium.

'There's hardly anyone here, Andy', he said. 'The gates are wide open. We could just walk in. In fact, I have just walked in. I'm standing by the corner flag right now. Comes out very easily. Might look good above your fireplace.'

'There's got to be something happening,' I said. 'I went to get the tickets. It definitely says 6pm. And the Bulgarians are here. I know, I saw them outside Top Shop.'

'Wait a minute, I can see someone down the other end,' Marcus went on. Perhaps it was Geir, I thought, Knattspyrnusamband Island's all-round Mr Fix-It. 'He's down by the other goal. Looks like he's putting up one of the nets. So I guess the game's on then.'

When I got back to the stadium ten minutes later, a van was unloading Icelandic footy merchandise - mainly boxes of velvet Viking novelty helmets in the correct shades of red, blue and white. One of Iceland's three policemen was asleep in a car by the open main gate. But there was still a distinct shortage of anyone who looked like a fan.

It didn't take long for the three of us to decide that, in the absence of, for example, any beer, or witty chanting by hordes of rival fans, we'd be better off out of the wind in a cafe just up the hill. Over a cake and a large coffee, we could see the stadium from the window. After a while we saw the Bulgarian team bus arrive, and then drive away again five minutes later, with everyone still on board and looking worried in case they really had chosen the wrong day to be here. Maybe Geir had lost the changing room key, or had forgotten to put up the other net. But they came back after another few minutes, just as the two countries' flags were hoisted up stadium poles, and at last the place began to look a bit lively.

YOU COME WITH ME - I GET TICKETS

With half an hour to go before kick-off we took our seats in the second row of the still half-empty main grandstand, and waited. There were a few Bulgarian ads around the perimeter, which was reassuring, as whatever game we were about to see was therefore likely to have some Bulgarian players in it and be of interest to the folks back home in Sofia.

Steve lives in Walton-on-Thames, in Surrey, and is a middle manager with four children, but surprisingly in those circumstances, he doesn't support Manchester United. Instead, he's a Watford fan. He set about knocking Iceland's national stadium.

'This place isn't much cop,' he moaned. 'Even Vicarage Road is a bigger ground than this.' This was true, but not totally fair, as Watford's population is probably bigger than Iceland's, and getting to the match is a bit easier when your only obstacle is the one-way system on the A412, as opposed to active volcanoes or ice-fields the size of Wales. The Laugardalsvollur stadium felt like one of the newer, better appointed grounds in the Nationwide League, sort of Rushden and Diamonds only without as many stands. The plastic bucket seats in the main stand, which was only about 12 rows deep, were almost comfortable. There were a few thousand seats opposite, but only grass banks behind each goal. After the heavy security I'd encountered in oppressive or just monstrously big stadiums like the Luzhniki in Moscow, the Olympic Stadium in Athens and the Ghencea stadium in Bucharest, it was a welcome change to come here and find a ground where the authorities only needed one policeman, you could leave your car right outside the main entrance to the ground and, if you wanted to, wander off and sit on a grass bank to watch your country play in the World Cup.

Helsinki-style Scandinavian chic clearly dictates that you don't turn up early for football in Iceland. Or maybe it's just too windy to sit around creating an atmosphere in competition with force nine gales. Not till ten to six did things get busy, by which time a fair-sized crowd had sauntered in, often in family groups of three or four, and had sat down as if it was Saturday afternoon at the local theatre. The game kicked off while some spectators were still arriving. By the time they'd finished arriving fashionably late, the game was a quarter over, but six or seven thousand people were in the ground. That's 4% of the population - the equivalent of two million people going to watch an England game. And yet this stadium could accommodate as many again. If it wasn't full for a game like this, when would it be? You couldn't see Valur Reykjavik versus Akranes pulling in the crowds.

Just before kick-off, desperate for something to notice, I started to walk round the ground. Bulgarian TV had wheeled out what looked like a former player, and he was being interviewed near the gate where the policeman was still in his car (and sitting upright, so at least local Law Enforcement was reassuringly awake). Bulgarian TV's expert summariser was being interviewed, Andy Gray-style, on a bit of grass about five yards away from where everyone else was walking to their seats, but not a single local succumbed to the temptation to stand behind him pulling silly faces or waving to Mum. It was the kind of place where Mum was probably already in her seat in the stands, bless her, or maybe she was selling the fantas and hot dogs you could buy once all your soft velvet multi-coloured Viking helmet requirements had been met.

I went to ask the interviewee who he was.

'I am Tushansky. I was a libero - you say sweeper. I played 20 times for my country.'

'Do you always work for Bulgarian TV?'

'No', he said, 'I am here to spy.' Normally, if a Bulgarian tells you he's a spy, you look around very carefully to see if any sharp, poison-tipped umbrellas are pointed anywhere near the backs of your legs. I'd be OK, I thought; there was a policeman five yards away, after all, and he might be glad of something to do. But even to Bulgarians, spying at football matches usually means looking for new talent. He told me he was the coach at Union Berlin, and was hoping to offer a contract to one or two up-and-coming Bulgarian - or even Icelandic - players.

It was national anthem time. Iceland's is wordless; either that or the locals are just too cool to bother singing it. As you'd expect, Bulgaria's was played to total, respectful silence from the local fans. Then the man on the PA (it sounded like Geir again to me) read out the teams: eleven players all with names ending in 'sson' up against eleven players all with names ending in 'ov'. I found myself thinking that if the playing surface cut up rough, it would be a sson ov a pitch to play on.

Iceland exerted heavy pressure early on, finding a lot of space, and they deservedly went a goal up. A ripple of polite applause went round the stand. The two lads in the seats alongside the three of us showed the most emotion, which was surprising, as they turned out not to be Icelandic. They were English. One of them, Pete, explained a bit long-sufferingly that he was in the country because his mate Gavin was mad about everything to do with Iceland. They'd gone to see Iceland's game against France a year or two earlier in Paris, which Iceland lost 3-2. You could be confident that Gavin would know how to treat his fiancee. 'For our honeymoon, darling, I'm taking you to see Iceland. At Wembley.'

At half-time I went off for some coffees to warm us up on this sunny mid-summer evening. As protection from the weather, the walkway behind the main stand had a glass roof and windows all the way down to the ground. You'd think Iceland was a pretty healthy and eco-conscious place, but over half the people standing down here were smoking and chucking their styrofoam coffee cups on the floor once they'd finished with them. In Moscow the riot police crunch you for doing that.

Perhaps Iceland took an early bath, or an early relaxing hot tub, at half-time because things went downhill badly for them in the second half. They had plenty more chances, but sent every one of them high, wide, or both. They became frustrated and the game turned niggly. The Bulgarian no. 4 went in with his foot high, which the locals weren't happy with at all - I could swear I heard one or two sharp intakes of breath. In the end a total of four yellow cards were waved in various faces, and there probably shouldn't have been all 22 players still on the pitch at the final whistle. Iceland did have one or two good shouts for a penalty turned down, to the increasingly vocal dissatisfaction of even this crowd. I asked Pete who the ref was.

'It's Dermot Gallagher from the English Premiership,' he said immediately, 'and he was right - there's no way that was a penalty.' Gavin might have been here to support Iceland, but clearly Pete was here to support some wonderful English refereeing.

'Afram Island! Afram Island!' sang the locals in an attempt to galvanise their team. It didn't work. Bulgaria pulled the goal back on 80 minutes, and their players ran along the front of the main stand, each with a hand ironically cupped to an ear, a sarcastic gesture common enough in England but one which this crowd seemed really shocked by. It's too nice a country for that kind of thing.

Iceland had the not inconsiderable wind behind them in the second half. Every goalkick from their end was landing in the penalty area at the other, and you could see, one by one, the Icelandic players losing patience and hoofing everything high and long on the off-chance that someone might make it forward in time to get on the end of it. But it didn't work and it finished 1-1. Both countries' campaigns probably ended there and then, despite Iceland's surprising win over the Czechs three months later. In the end, only Denmark were to reach the finals from this qualifying group.

There hadn't been a stampede to get in, but at the end it seemed as if everyone wanted to forget about the game as quickly as possible. All the advertising boards had been knocked down and the stand was two-thirds empty, even before Icelandic TV had finished interviewing Hermann Hreidarsson - then of Ipswich - on his way off the pitch. The crowd had done their best to create an atmosphere, but with the climate, and such a small footballing public, it doesn't take much to work out why clubs in countries like England end up with all the country's playing talent.

Thanks to the ticket in my pocket, I knew I'd been at a game, but 10 minutes after the final whistle the car park was as empty as at 2.30 that afternoon, as if the game hadn't really happened after all. The three of us went off to a fish restaurant (I'd obviously wasted my time in town this morning then) for a meal and before very long, we were talking about other things. Like, 'that salmon costs how much?'

Next day, with no other transport and only half a day left, I went on a coach tour - you can get quite a few of the sights (geysers, waterfalls, old Viking parliaments, that kind of thing) ticked off in just a few hours. As is the way in Iceland, cars come round to the hotels to collect the pre-booked passengers and take them out to the coach station. Two Swedish lads and I were in a little Fiat driven by a spiky-haired local. One of the Swedes leaned forward to ask him the score in the game last night.

'I was there,' I said helpfully. 'It was 1-1.'

'Who to?' asked the driver.

12.

In Tbilisi We Have Not Footboll!!

Georgia - Hungary, Lokomotivi Stadium, Tbilisi, Saturday 1 September 2001

THAT SATURDAY NIGHT when Michael Owen scored a hat trick in England's 5-1 rout of Germany, I wasn't in the pub, or at home, or at a friend's house. I wasn't even round at the in-laws having to watch repeats of 'Stars in Their Eyes'. Where I was, the time difference meant it was after midnight by the time the second half in Munich was under way, and I was watching the goals go in, over a beer and a chicken shashlik, in a hotel basement in Tbilisi in the silent company of the night security man.

Technically, Georgia isn't really in Europe, being south of the Caucasus mountains, but former Soviet giants like Dinamo Tbilisi, past winners of the UEFA Cup, bring a European feel to the country's football. For this World Cup, Georgia were in Italy's group, but hadn't exactly set it alight so far with goals and audacious play. Neither had Italy, to be fair. Neither do Italy ever, to be even fairer.

Hungary, however, would be well up for it. They really needed to win this game in Tbilisi, which I fancied them to do, and that would then nicely set up their home game with Romania in Budapest four days later. They had to get the two wins if they were to have a chance of second place and a play-off. To come second themselves, Georgia needed to win all their last three games, score dozens of goals and rely on just about everyone else to lose at least twice. It looked more likely that England would trounce the Germans 5-1 than that Georgia would pull that one off.

At club level, Georgian football has been marooned by the break-up of the USSR, which has meant that, at national level, Georgia have turned out to be more winned against than winning. However, they did warm up for this game with a comfortable 3-0 victory in Luxembourg in August, in front of a massive crowd of 700 fans. The new Georgian coach, Alex Chivadze, a veteran defender from 1980s USSR days, had had to field a weakened side in that game, as Lokomotiv Moscow striker Zaza Janashia was reportedly selected but ignored the call-up. Chivadze promptly omitted him from the squad to play Hungary and Romania.

To fans of those few British clubs who've never had either Georgi Kinkladze or Temuri Ketsbaia on their books, Georgia is no more than one of those countries Northern Ireland always seem to get drawn against. They go out there, complain that the practice facilities aren't good enough for their superstar Nationwide League players, play out a 1-0, losing as often as not, and come home again. But football is a way of life in Georgia, and local teams have known real success, albeit in the less moneyed USSR era. Dinamo Tbilisi's 1981 UEFA Cup-winning squad are still on display, on a big poster in the National Stadium. Chivadze, a member of that team, was merely one of many Georgians to feature regularly in the USSR line-up.

Political independence was declared in 1991, although it was achieved less peacefully than in other, luckier, ex-Soviet republics. A number of violent incidents led to a two-week street shoot-out in December that year, as rebels ousted Zviad Gamsakhurdia's government. Gamsakhurdia took refuge in Chechnya, of all places, which says a thing or two about him.

With a 30% win record in the decade to 2001, the new republic's footballers have probably done as well as anyone would have thought, and considerably better than some other outposts of the former USSR. But of the two teams due to meet on September 1, Hungary had by far the more realistic chance of making it to Japan/Korea.

IN TBILISI WE HAVE NOT FOOTBOLL!!

As they weren't charging anything like the $48 that the people at the Aerostar in Moscow had wanted, I asked the hotel to send a car to the airport to pick me up. It was a Soviet-era Lada, from which the seat-belts had been removed, probably deliberately, and the wipers had been nicked. The one factory-fitted wing mirror was also missing. The speedo was bust, but that didn't really matter, as in Georgia whether your speedo's working or not doesn't alter the price of fish very much. I could have bought this car for $48, never mind just had a ride from the airport in the thing.

As for the seat belts, anywhere east of the European Union they're strictly for wimps. If your car isn't being driven by a wimp, you don't wear a seat belt, because to do so insults the driver's manhood. It's as simple as that. And not many Georgian drivers are wimps. So far, Georgians haven't seen the connection between the high numbers of people involuntarily, and fatally, leaving their cars through the front windscreen and the low national level of seat belt use. You feel like giving them a piece of paper with '2' and '2' written on it and saying, 'Have you tried adding these two numbers together?'

'My car is available for tours,' said the driver encouragingly as we rattled into town. As befits a country where the Russians, or at least the Soviets, built most of the roads, there are plenty of two or three-lane dual carriageways, but the potholes reduce the usable part of the road to a kind of racing line, often requiring the use of all three lanes in a given 50-yard stretch of tarmac.

And that's the main roads - the side roads are far worse. On them the pothole is the road, as I saw a couple of days later when I had a free day and hired another driver in a marginally better car (a 10-year old Audi 80 that had to be hot-wired into starting each time), to take me into the mountains. Muraz was a chain-smoking, sun-worshipping Kurd who thought nothing of using the outside of hairpin bends to cut up carloads full of dodgy-looking blokes heading north over the border into bandit country in Chechnya and southern Russia. Nor was he too bothered about ravines, slow-moving on-road livestock or sudden total brake failure at the bottom of a hill. To keep my mind from dwelling on the high chance of a gravity-assisted heavy-impact end to my time on earth,

YOU COME WITH ME - I GET TICKETS

I compiled a list of Questions You'll Most Want To Ask A Georgian Driver.

1. Shall I explain what that pedal in the middle is for?
2. If you trail your arm out the window the whole time while we go round these hairpin bends, how long does it take for that cigarette to burn to the end?
3. Are you sure you meant to let that old peasant woman cross the road?
4. Are you aware that touching two wires together to start the car is slightly non-standard?
5. As that's a 500ft ravine on your side, shall we let that oil tanker go by before you try and overtake this truck?
6. What with the potholes and everything, do you think if we went a bit slower we wouldn't keep whacking our heads on the doorframe?
7. Did you deliberately remove the seatbelts so that no one would criticise your performance in bed, or did they just fall off from disuse?
8. Was that your oil warning light that came on an hour ago?

Although I was mainly in Georgia for the football, I was also researching an article about the country's rugby, so I spent part of my first evening in Tbilisi and all of the following afternoon, a Saturday, in a Georgian cable TV studio, with Zaal Guiguineishvili, the country's most experienced rugby commentator. The game on Saturday was Australia against the All Blacks in John Eales' last ever game. Strange as it may sound, rugby is nearly as popular in Georgia as football (so is Formula 1, which may explain the driving habits). The national rugby side, known as the Lelos, were voted Georgian Team of the Decade of Independence at the end of 2001, and were looking much more likely to reach their respective World Cup finals than the football lot - which is how things turned out.

BBC Television Centre it wasn't. Zaal's cable company had one small studio, and all its receivers were in a separate room on the floor above, connected to a couple of satellite dishes on the roof.

IN TBILISI WE HAVE NOT FOOTBOLL!!

The rest of the building was a local government office, whose officials were probably making ends meet by renting out a bit of space to the TV people. Behind the building was a post-nuclear type wasteland of concrete, twisted metal, abandoned vehicles, ramshackle sheds and large items of heavy machinery, all of which looked unused since 1991. Aussie no.8 Toutai Kefu crashed against the posts for the match-winning try as a technician behind me watched Sigourney Weaver in the original Alien on another screen.

I got up to go back to the place where I was staying. It's impossible to pigeon-hole Tbilisi, but here goes anyway. It's part industrialised world, part developing world, part East Europe, part Asia, part Middle-East and, on a bad day, such as when bullets fly (constantly, early 1990s), the entire cabinet is sacked by the President (October 2001), or power stations explode (December 2001), or when the President is overthrown by the entire Cabinet (December 2003), it has more than a twist of Latin-American dictatorship about it. Georgia was the second country in the world, after Armenia, to embrace Christianity. Traditional values and a deep sense of family honour persist, as do long memories of scores to be settled or debts to be paid. Right opposite McDonalds is the Iveria hotel, an Intourist showpiece in Soviet days, but now home to hundreds if not thousands of refugees from Georgia's civil war with Abkhazian separatists. Meanwhile, most urban teenagers and twenty-something women look and even dress like Italians, and some of the older men could almost pass for English, right down to the flat caps, V-neck pullovers and socks-with-sandals. They are, literally, Caucasian, and you can see familiar white male balding patterns and Bobby Charlton-style wrap-around hairdos everywhere you look.

Zaal offered to walk me back to where I had to catch my taxi-bus. This was helpful, as all signs and street names are in Georgian only, and Georgian is written in the kind of alphabet that makes Chinese look like you really could pick it up in three weeks while driving to work on the M25. Luckily, Zaal's English was excellent. I asked him what he, as a rugby fan, thought of Georgian football.

'They're sissies,' he said. I thought he just meant that the country's soccer players would call for jumbo-sized Pampers if you threatened to put them anywhere near the bottom of a ruck or the front row of a scrum, but he was just referring to their way of life. He thought the country's top players were softies, interested just in themselves, driving Ferraris and making a mint playing for elite West European clubs (that would be clubs like Derby, Wolves and Dundee, then. Not to mention mighty FC Zurich, who have the brilliantly named Gocha Jamarauli on their books). Zaal had told me that all Georgia's top rugby players play professionally in France, but somehow that was OK, while top footballing talent doing the same thing was not.

Maybe Zaal's problem was more to do with the balance of power between the two sports. When independence was declared, football had what money there was and grabbed all the best facilities, marginalising rugby to a few ramshackle grounds on the outskirts of town. In March that year, with a World Cup qualifier against Romania coming up, the Georgian FA had leaned on the Georgian RU to switch an international match to another city so as to protect the playing surface in the Lokomotivi stadium for the footballers. 'Our FA said their players were so talented they needed a surface like for billiards,' said Zaal scathingly, 'but Romania played them off the park. Then Georgia's rugby heroes won against Romania a month later.'

Before I left to come home, Zaal took me on a tour of the country's rugby facilities, such as they were. On one ground, refugees from Abkhazia were grazing their donkeys and chickens inside the 22. At another, the scrum half, who doubled as the club barman, poured me a pint even though it was barely 10am. It's good to see some rugby traditions are global.

Zaal was nothing if not protective. I was not to use the metro, he said, as it was filthy, full of pickpockets and suffered regular power cuts. As we crossed over an intersection where all the roads were 50 yards wide, I told him of my plans to visit the mountains a couple of days after the Hungary game. 'Don't go,' he said, 'it will be very dangerous for you.'

It was a wonder Zaal ever went anywhere himself. Maybe he was thinking of hairpin bends above enormous ravines, without any of those nice crash barriers so thoughtfully provided in the West.

'Do you mean because of the roads? The driving in the mountains?'

'No,' he said. 'There are bandits. They are always looking out for foreigners.' I knew Chechnya wasn't far away, but it was on the northern, Russian side of the mountains. As far as I knew, Chechnya and Georgia weren't actually at each other's throats.

'Look,' said Zaal and pointed to a huge advertising hoarding above our heads, with one blank section where an advertisement had just been taken down. 'Until this week, there has been an advertisement there, appealing for help. It was to find an Austrian businessman, who was kidnapped in June. He was working for the UN. Many, many times this happens.'

'So who's doing it?' I asked. 'It can't be the Chechens.'

'Some people say, Georgian Police and Government.'

In June 2002, a senior British banker was kidnapped in the centre of Tbilisi by a gang obviously well aware not only of his movements, but also that he was due to return to the UK for good two days later, after six years in Tbilisi. It wasn't until November that he was freed, by a unit of the Georgian army. The brother of Kakha Kaladze, a Georgian player due to appear against Hungary in the game I was there to see, has not yet been so lucky. His club, AC Milan, are rumoured to have paid $600,000 for his brother's release. If they did pay that as a ransom, it hasn't worked.

For Zaal, there would be too many riotous teenagers at the football. He bought a couple of tickets for me - actually match programmes, which doubled as tickets by having a block, row and seat number written on in biro. What with the teenagers, and the prima donna soccer players, he wasn't that interested in going himself, but had strongly advised me to go with someone for my own safety. After I'd got to Tbilisi and seen the place for myself, I could make the judgement that he was exaggerating any danger that there might have been to an unimportant temporary visitor like me. At the time, I took him at his word and went about contacting one or two fans before leaving the UK, just in case he was right. I found a website on Georgian football run by Stuart, a Scottish Manchester City supporter who must have been at Maine Road one of the times Kinkladze had a good game. He gave me a few names of people he knew in Tbilisi. At random, I contacted Dato and asked him what he thought about the game coming up.

'Every who wont can f**k our plaiers!' Dato surprisingly informed me in the first line of his reply. 'They now everything but they do not nou football! I hate the Georgian football! In Tbilisi we have not footboll!!! F**k tha Georgian football!! I thinck, you anderstand me!!' Well, not much room for ambiguity there, all in all, despite the spelling. If that was what he thought, was he going to bother to go to the game himself? Yes, he said, of course he was.

It's never wise to judge too much by first impressions, but I was slightly in two minds as to whether Dato qualified as the reliable, stable kind of chap I needed to keep me safe from the hordes of police and government mountain bandits waiting to kidnap me. The only way to find out was to arrange to meet him. This would involve beer.

'I like bear very much and when you come we drinck a lot of bear. Do you know what is Kinkali and Kababi?' I didn't, but it would be interesting to find out. 'Georgian plaiers are not football plaiers, I thinck they are motherf*****s!!' Clearly Zaal was not alone in his assessment of the country's footballers, although Dato's viewpoint was a little less cogently presented.

The other person on Stuart's list who I tried to contact was called Rati. Rati's Dad turned out to be the Programme Controller for Georgian State TV, while Rati himself was earning megabucks working for the Georgian International Oil Company - in particular the $4bn pipeline across Georgia to take Caspian crude to the Black Sea (see James Bond 007 in 'The World Is Not Enough' for in-depth geo-political analysis of this issue). Thanks to Daddy, Rati had two tickets for the Press Box, and offered one to me, which sounded like a good deal. Dato had said that he and his chum Dima already had tickets, so I said I'd meet them for plenty of bear the day after the game, and took up Rati's offer.

Rati picked me up from the place I was staying a couple of hours before kick-off. He drove a 6-year old Lada Niva, which had seatbelts, although I wasn't allowed to put mine on, and off we went to the slightly worryingly named 'Excess Bar' for something to eat. He told me he was 25, he'd been to Turkey dozens of times on business, his brother worked in the Georgian consulate in Istanbul, and he was just about to take his girlfriend (his own, not his brother's) to some Turkish resort like Antalya for a week's sand and sex. Meanwhile, he was prepared to slum it with the likes of me at the football tonight. Once he'd finished telling me what a great life he had, we talked about tonight's game. Georgian crowds weren't all as down on their team as Dato and Zaal, he said. Just most of them. They might start off enthusiastic enough, but if it was still 0-0 after half an hour, or if Georgia went behind, the booing would kick in pretty soon afterwards.

Unfortunately the jobsworths on the gate to the Press Box wouldn't let Rati in, so he had to slum it even more by coming in on the tickets Zaal had bought for me. Quite late on, the Hungary game had been switched from the 80,000 capacity Boris Paichadze national stadium to the Lokomotivi stadium, capacity 25,000 or so, possibly once it was clear that ticket sales wouldn't even half fill the national stadium. As it turned out, the Lokomotivi itself was only half full: evidently the locals here had no intention of turning out to support their team if their chances of qualification were thinner than a student's wallet after graduation. This contrasted with the country's Lelos rugby side, who were regularly winning - and packing in crowds of 30,000 or 40,000 for internationals. Maybe Georgians are just glory-hunters when it comes to sport. Maybe we all are.

The kick-off was 9pm, but it only got dark just before the teams came out, and a full moon rose into a clear sky from behind the hills to the south-east. The crowd was so relaxed they remained seated and determinedly chain-smoked through their own country's national anthem. September it may have been, but summer was lingering and the day had been languid and hot. You could buy fresh-baked and tantalisingly aromatic ciabatta-style bread to munch on as you watched, as well as four different kinds of seeds to eat out of a cone made of old newspaper. We spotted one lad walking up and down selling books of his own poems, something which probably wouldn't work too well at, say, the New Den.

YOU COME WITH ME - I GET TICKETS

The Lokomotivi is a natural amphitheatre, more of a bowl than a stadium. It had been refurbished to UEFA standards only a year or two previously, which meant it had to have plastic bucket seats instead of the old wooden benches that give you splinters in the bum. A couple of practice pitches and a hotel were still under construction, which when finished would make the complex a well-appointed one. It was near Vake Park, one of the smartest areas of Tbilisi.

At least the Georgians, in Kinkladze, Glasgow Rangers' Shota Arveladze, and Kakha Kaladze of AC Milan, had a few household (OK, maybe not quite) names in their starting line-up, however dim a view of them the Georgian crowd took. If Kinkladze came in for the most stick from the fans, Temuri Ketsbaia would have run him close, had he been playing. Sadly, the grandaddy of the squad - he was in his early 30s - was crocked and had to sit the game out.

Hungarian football seemed also to have fallen on hard times. In England we always think back to Wembley, 1953, and the 6-3 drubbing the Hungarians handed out to us that day, the first time England had ever been beaten at home, and somehow we still think that the country should be a force in the game, but for decades this has been true only intermittently (such as in August 2002, when Zalaegerszeg registered their memorable 1-0 win against Manchester United, only to get ripped to bits at Old Trafford a fortnight later). All but three of Hungary's 20-man squad were based abroad, but these other seventeen would typically play for Israeli or former East German clubs, apart from central defender Shaba Feher, who had managed to end up with no less a club than KFC Verbroidering Geel of Belgium.

According to Rati, 70,000 had seen Georgia's game against Italy in the summer, but 12,000 at best were here tonight. They weren't shouting, they weren't even singing their own anthem, and they were too laid back to boo or whistle during Hungary's. Georgia squandered three or four good chances in the first half hour, after which even this docile crowd began to get on their backs, as Rati had predicted. Then Shota Arveladze put Georgia one up after 35 minutes, only for the Hungarians to level just before half-time, springing an off-side trap to put the ball past Gvaramadze in the Georgian goal.

IN TBILISI WE HAVE NOT FOOTBOLL!!

Then the second half was all Georgia. Chivadze brought on Giorgi Demetradze, of Real Sociedad, and he tore the Hungarian defence apart every few minutes. Gocha Jamarauli re-established Georgia's lead, and then Demetradze set up Georgia's third. The crowd woke up, the team took a bow after the final whistle, and the Georgian players were so motivated by their own success that they had a player sent off for what looked like over-celebration of the third goal. He came over to the security fence in front of the block Rati and I were in and nearly shook it out of the ground. As he'd been a naughty boy once in the game already, this was his second yellow, so off he had to go. At the same time as being a convincing Georgian win, the 3-1 result also more or less killed off Hungary's chances of qualifying.

Rati dropped me off at my hotel afterwards. They knew I was going to be late and they'd kindly offered to do me a meal whenever I got back. Because of the 3-hour time difference between Georgia and Germany, I was in time to catch most of England's game in Munich, including Michael Owen's second and third goals, over that chicken shashlik in the night security man's room. Thanks to Georgian commentary over German TV pictures, I can inform any German readers who may be interested that the Georgian for 'Michael Owen hat trick' is 'Michaeli Oweni hat trick'.

On Sunday, I met up with Dato and Dima. They were both students in Tbilisi, and Real Madrid and AC Milan fans respectively. Dato had been an open-side flanker as well, in the 15-man code of football. I pointed out to him that for a team of motherf*****s, Georgia had played rather well last night. They had to agree that it had been Georgia's best performance for some time. It was only Aleksandr Chivadze's second game in charge, after the friendly in Luxembourg, and the signs for the future were looking good. After the sending off, they thought Georgia had played even better, despite being a player down, and for them Demetradze had been superb. 'He should be in the starting line-up from now on,' said Dato.

But they were much more interested in Western European football than anything domestic. England's win the night before was very popular with these guys. 'The Germans play only to win,' they said, as if that was an unexpected thing to do. Then it was time to pump me for information. Among other things, they wanted to know who I supported, who my favourite defender was, what I thought of Sven-Goran Eriksson, what about this or that Liverpool performance, and who I fancied for the Champions' League. For them, the start of the Champions' League on September 11 (just nine days away - little did any of us know at the time) was the main footballing event to look forward to now. Dima was upset, because had Dinamo Tbilisi managed not to get themselves knocked out of the UEFA Cup by a club from Malta in the first and only qualifying round, they would have landed a plum tie against his adopted team, AC Milan.

Face to face, these guys were of course far less wild than Dato's e-mails had superficially made them seem. If anything they were a bit serious about life and their football. We only dranck three bears. They wanted their national team to show more commitment: it was fine for the players to get personally rich by playing for their clubs abroad, but when they came home for internationals, it was time to play with patriotism and passion. This echoed Zaal's views as well; he thought the Lelos rugby players were fired up by playing for their country, in a way that the footballers were not. 80% of Georgian men followed football, said Dato, except during major tournaments, when it was 100%. I asked if women followed the game too. 'No,' they said. 'They're in the kitchen.' I hoped they were joking there, but I wasn't sure. Rati had told me it was just about considered acceptable to bring your wife or girlfriend to the game. 'But they don't love football.'

'You always have friends in Georgia,' they told me as they took me back to where I was staying, which was well out of their way. Such is the unfailing courtesy and consideration afforded to visitors by all Georgians, provided that they're neither policemen nor bandits, that so far I'd been accompanied to or from the door of the hotel nearly every time I'd gone anywhere or done anything. The hotel was quite small, and apart from me was otherwise full of businessmen and UN-type economics people. Although I'd been there nearly three days, I hadn't yet met or even seen a single other resident, as the hours I was keeping weren't really in synch with the schedules of economic observer life.

The next morning was my last full day in the country, the day for Muraz to drive me up into the mountains. Muraz knew his football and kept me up to date with all the latest 'Juve offer $70 million for Owen' rumours that were emerging in the aftermath of England's win in Munich on Saturday. He also reminded me that if we carried on over the mountains we'd come out near the neighbouring Russian Republic of Dagestan. It was Russian in name only: in terms of visitor safety you couldn't put a cigarette paper between it and Chechnya. Around this time, Glasgow Rangers (known locally, inevitably, as Rangers Glasgow) were drawn to play Makhachkala, on the Caspian coast of Dagestan. They refused to travel and eventually UEFA ruled that the game should be played on neutral territory.

After about 273 hairpin bends we made it to Gergeti, a village in the shadow of Mount Kazbeg. Kazbeg is snow-capped all year and, at 17,000 feet high, is of the same national significance to the Georgians as the Matterhorn is to the Swiss. I wanted to see Tsminda Sameba, a stunningly located church on a ridge a few miles south of the mountain, so I had Muraz drive me through the village to the end of the path, gave him a couple of hours off, and found Genri, one of a group of shepherds, who was prepared to guide me up through the woods for a few lari. The faded green canvas cap on Genri's head said, 'Dinamo Batumi'. The shiny new red and white plastic carrier bag my guidebook and 3.1 megapixel digital camera were in said, 'Austrian Airlines Vienna: Shopping Like Heaven - Buy More For Less'. I was so obviously from a different planet I felt like asking him to take me to his leader. Except that this man looked like he was their leader already.

Muraz was asleep when I got back down the hill. On the way back to Tbilisi he managed not to get stopped at any of the police checkpoints - it was always the car just in front or just behind us that was pulled over. He was obviously a lucky man, so I got him to drive me to the airport the next day for the flight back to Vienna.

YOU COME WITH ME - I GET TICKETS

I was sorry to leave. Georgian food is fantastic, the people invariably friendly and, despite the events of June 2002, extremely unlikely to kidnap you; and if they can ever keep enough money out of the pockets of corrupt officials to get a sound economy going, the place has everything going for it: a wonderful climate, mountains, beaches, scenery, wine, thousands of years of history, and only one McDonalds.

The following year, Dima contacted me again, from Claridges hotel in London. Well OK, he was there as a waiter while studying to improve his English, and if there was a big do on, like Joan Collins' fifth wedding for example, he would have no option but to work a 16 hour day from 11am until 3 the next morning, but it was still quite a place to be. So one weekend, shortly before the World Cup, we arranged to meet in central London to see a Fulham game at Loftus Road. He was with a friend of his called Shalva, who happened to be his best mate from school and who happened to be working at Claridges as well.

In a Soho bar, after the game and over the first three pound pints I'd ever bought, they blew cigarette smoke in my face from point blank range and told me about how Georgians in London looked after one another. There are 10,000 Georgians in London. I don't know about the other 9,996, but I can reveal that as of early May 2002, four of them were working in Claridges, three of them thanks to Shalva, and that all four had been there until the small hours the night before, as Claridges had hosted a major society wedding which had numbered Elton John among the guests. Gin and tonics were the standard Claridges eight pounds a time.

'Endrew.' Shalva waved at me to lean forward into a not exactly morning-fresh cloud of exhaled Camel smoke. Between them, these two had demolished three-quarters of a pack in 40 minutes and didn't look like slowing down. 'Have you seen the penthouses in Claridges?'

'No. Places like that are a bit out of my range. And I've never met Joan Collins.'

'Five thousand. Five thousand pounds a night. Churchill stay there. And Rostropovich, the great kompozitor.' Maybe he meant

IN TBILISI WE HAVE NOT FOOTBOLL!!

Shostakovich, the great kompozitor, that is if Stalin ever let him out of the USSR.

Shalva was still talking. 'You get two rooms, bathroom with jacuzzi, and big balkon.'

'A big what?'

'A big balkon. You can sit there. For fantastic view over London.'

It was one of the last match days of the Italian season and Dima asked if I knew the scores. His team, AC Milan, were going for fourth place in Serie A and a probable Champions' League spot. I told him I hadn't heard the results, in a way which I hope made him think I usually would have known. He let me off, as his mobile rang just then. It was his mum from Tbilisi, at what must have been around two in the morning over there. My Georgian still wasn't too good, but I think I heard him say he had enough clean socks for that week.

Despite a number of phone calls and e-mails, I never saw or heard from Dima, Dato or Shalva again. Rati stayed in touch for a while. Later in 2002, when Georgia were playing a Rugby World Cup qualifier against Ireland at Lansdowne Road, I got an Irish RFU Press Pass on the slightly spurious basis that I was doing a match report for Zaal to use in the Georgian media, which in fact I did write. Then, in the months before the Rugby World Cup in autumn 2003, Zaal also went to ground. But all of these people helped me enormously and showed me humbling hospitality when I was in their country, and I wish them well.

13.

Why You See This Game?

'WHY YOU SEE this game?' Laszlo wanted to know.

I was really beginning to wonder myself. I'd arrived in Budapest at lunchtime, after stopping off in Vienna on my way back from Georgia. It had been pouring with rain as I left the railway station and, six hours later and near kick-off time, the Nep Stadium pitch was likely to be so flooded that if a manager brought on a sub you'd have to look closely to see if it had legs or propellers. And by losing so expertly to Georgia in Tbilisi at the weekend, Hungary had effectively removed any semblance of competitive edge from the game that was due to start in about an hour or so.

Since seeing that first game in Helsinki just over a year previously, I'd seen 11 games and 22 different teams. Yet here, I was about to watch a team not just for the second time, but for the second time in four days. If that team had been Brazil or even England, you might not have minded too much, especially as this game was just four days after that result in Munich. But it wasn't, it was Hungary.

The fact was, I'd taken a punt on this one, and lost. If Hungary had won in Georgia, which on form to date had been on the cards, this game in Budapest would have been an all-out slugfest for second place between two not terribly friendly Balkan neighbours. This Carpathian rivalry had been what attracted me to this game in the first place, rather than, say, the big Liechtenstein-Spain clash in Vaduz, down the road the other way from Vienna. As it was,

WHY YOU SEE THIS GAME?

Hungary's defeat at the weekend had left them with too much ground to make up, and meant instead that Romania had an armchair ride into second place and a play-off spot.

All in all, this game was likely to have about as much bite as Dolly the Sheep in a retirement home. Mathematically, it was still possible for Hungary to qualify behind Italy for a play-off spot, but there would have to be a whole series of silly results: they would have to win tonight and then beat Italy away, while relying on Georgia to wallop the Romanians themselves. It wasn't going to happen, and you could sense that everyone in this damp, draughty bus shelter knew it. This bus shelter was the only place within a mile of the stadium, including the stadium itself, that was undercover, and so it was packed.

I took the opportunity to have a beer, having just made a lucky purchase - nothing less than one of the last 65,000 unsold tickets for tonight's game. Laszlo and his chums were on the other side of the stand-up counter from me. It was wet, windy and cold, we were all standing in one of those tarmac rainwater puddles that have lurid purple and yellow oil slicks on the surface, and every 30 seconds or so a huge, fume-belching bus would arrive or leave from the stop about three yards behind Laszlo's head. The noise (mainly my chattering teeth, as I was still dressed for late summer in the Caucasus) and one or two mutual language difficulties made conversation a little stilted. I'd not managed to pick up Hungarian since lunchtime.

'Will Hungary win?' I asked Laszlo. Back came a resigned shrug. Best try another tack, I thought. Such as, um, English football. Everyone's got an opinion on that, haven't they?

'Was it good or bad for you when England beat Germany?'

'Huh?'

'You know, were you happy when England won?'

'Oh, happy, yes. Michael Ovin!'

OK, good. Here was one conversation that just wasn't going to develop. A pity really, as this was what I'd seen myself doing while travelling to these games. I'd wanted to find out what rank and file, so-called blue collar football followers, in unfashionable places, well away from the slick, UEFA-marketed, glamorous side of the game thought about football, their country's chances, what they felt about the opposition, and so forth. And here I had another real chance to do just that, but Laszlo couldn't understand me and I couldn't understand him. I got him to point out which entrance to the stadium I would need, and retreated into my beer bottle while he and his friends started talking among themselves. I stayed where I was. I didn't fancy getting any wetter by going outside.

By now, Imre had elbowed his way to the counter, alongside me. His English was slightly better: in fact he'd actually been to England, in 1997, at the time of Princess Diana's funeral. Whether he'd gone all the way to England just for that, or whether the Arsenal-Tottenham game he'd seen during his visit was more memorable, I couldn't quite tell. It had been 0-0 but he thought it was 'fantastic'. You felt that even a goalless English Premiership game meant more to him than, say, Ferencvaros against Honved in his own country.

For all Imre's better English, he had no tips to pass on about the result tonight, the size of the crowd, or even - my conversational ice-breaker in bus shelters like this - which entrance to the stadium I needed. So far I had solemnly listened while about four different people had all pointed out the same gate to me. There was a diagram on the back of the ticket as well, but I had to pretend I hadn't seen that or I'd have had nothing much to talk about.

Imre clapped me on the shoulder and left. It still wasn't kick-off time, so I hung around to finish my beer.

'Please. Really why you see this game?'

Laszlo was back. I took a deep breath. There wasn't much I could tell him.

The Nep stadium is massive, but the top tier was as yet unreconstructed - in other words, UEFA-approved, plastic bucket seats hadn't yet been installed up there. With a measly crowd of 8,000 tonight, however, that was hardly going to matter. Such fanatical Hungarian supporters as had decided to turn out were clustered behind each goal, each with a sodden red, white and green flag clinging tightly around their shoulders, like the losers in a Lads Only Club 18-30 Wet Flag competition. Apart from the VIPs, the entire stadium was exposed to the weather, and in the circumstances the noise these few aficionados made was pretty impressive, if you didn't mind them viciously booing the Romanian national anthem. It really isn't just English fans who do this kind of thing, and don't let anyone tell you different. So far Iceland was the only country, out of twelve, where it hadn't happened.

Ten minutes into the game, the police had to wade in with batons and tear gas when the fans at the far end of the ground from me threatened to get a bit close to the 300 or so Romanian fans sectored off in the adjoining block. It was all under control again in a couple of minutes. All that was more interesting to watch than the actual game, which Romania, with Gheorghe Hagi now in charge, won with ease. The rain never let up throughout the match. Matyus Janos, who'd scored Hungary's goal against Georgia, had two excellent chances early on and missed with both, although he did hit the post once. By the end, those 300 Romanians were outsinging the Hungarian crowd, many of whom spent the last 20 minutes cheering their own team's comical skids, slips and air-kicks. The conditions were bad, but the Romanian players weren't doing that.

I almost left before the end, which would have broken the promise I'd made to myself never to do that kind of thing. Real supporters do it for 90 minutes, but this game would have tested the resolve of even the most fanatical followers. When the final whistle did go, I was the first one out of the stadium. I thought about finding the bus stop again for a 'goodbye-Budapest-and-thanks-for-the-memories' bottle of fizzy beer, as the atmosphere in the stadium tonight had made the bus shelter look like one of Budapest's most convivial drinking joints. At least it had had a roof. But instead I just went back to my hotel to drip rainwater on to their carpet.

Not a memorable night, all in all. Perhaps the moral of the story was, don't make elaborate plans to cross half a continent to go to a game if its whole character depends on results not yet in. Next stop Zagreb, for a game that had had buckets of competitive meaning for months. Things could only get better, as they say.

14.

Dinamo Are Political Club

Croatia - Belgium, Maksimir Stadium, Zagreb, Saturday 6 October 2001

'CRIMES,' said Josip. 'Many war crimes.'

It was half-time in the Maksimir stadium, which was packed to the rafters with over 40,000 people (after the 8,000 in the Nep Stadium last month, that at least was good news). Josip had just told me he reckoned 70% of those people would have fought in the 1990s wars against Serbia or the Bosnian Muslims - Bosniaks - in some capacity or other. Certainly Josip had fought in these wars himself: he'd just told me that he'd been banged up in jail for a month by his own army.

The day before, when I met him in the office of the Croatian Football Federation, he'd had a fag in his mouth and his feet up on his girlfriend Vlatka's desk, listening to AC/DC and Led Zeppelin. By contrast, Vlatka had been foot-to-the-floor busy for weeks before this game. The game was a complete sell-out, and Vlatka's English was better than anyone else's in the CFF, and so she'd had to do plenty of foreign liaison.

It had been obvious since the summer that this game would sell out. The way things stood on the eve of the game, the winner would qualify directly, while the loser would face an unpredictable play-off. This was Scotland's group, but even if Craig Brown's team were to thump Latvia by a cricket score, they were out of it: everything hung on this fixture. Belgium could afford to draw, so the home team would have to make the running.

Vlatka had told me on the phone that she could help me, if I showed up in her office on the morning of the game. As it happened, I had found myself with time to spare the afternoon before, so I'd gone along on the off-chance that she was there.

The CFF building was a newish one, with red roof tiles like ten million or so others across Germany and central Europe. It was certainly better appointed inside than the Icelandic Federation's wooden hut, or the smoke-filled single room from which Georgian football is administered. In the reception area, a dozen or so people were waiting for what could have been Christmas, for all the urgency anyone was showing. Videos of old Croatian games - or at least games from Croatia's successful campaign in France '98 - were being played on a TV built into the wall. Once the receptionist had finished chatting on the phone I asked to see Vlatka. Actually knowing a name, or being foreign, got me straight to the head of the queue and I was shown into her office. In contrast to the lethargic scene outside, she was busy dealing with all manner of requests for tickets, like the one from a Japanese journalist who walked in soon after me. He was checking out Japan's likely opposition, knowing that definitely one (and as it turned out, both) of these teams would be making the journey to the Far East next June. Josip meanwhile was chilling out to classic 80s heavy metal.

'Rock 'n' Roll Ain't Noise Pollution', yelped AC/DC's Brian Johnson. Clearly this number was one of Josip's favourite tracks. He took his feet off her desk for a second or two, reached for the zap gun and cranked the volume up another notch or two, while Vlatka reached into a drawer and took out a wad of tickets. A ticket for the most important game in Croatia's season would cost me about two pounds, did I mind paying that much? I said if I pushed the boat out I could probably afford it, and was about to hand over the right number of Croatian kunas, when Josip offered me a ticket of his own, in the East Stand with him and alongside the real fans. Just in case Vlatka had been about to put me in with the Belgians, I jumped at Josip's offer. It's always better to go along with a local anyway.

Maybe because what I was doing was sufficiently different from the dozens of tired old football hacks just doing their job, or more likely because it was now 5 o'clock on a sunny Friday afternoon and the rush appeared to be over, Vlatka and Josip offered me a drink. She put her own feet up on the desk as well, took one of Josip's fags and lit up. She asked me how efficient the English FA were at organising games, obviously expecting me to know. I said something that I hoped would make it sound as if I had an informed opinion on the matter, when I didn't really.

Evidently she wasn't overly impressed with her own Federation's administrative capabilities. She said she had been there until 3am the night before fixing tickets for a range of junior clubs across Croatia, and accreditation for journalists from all over the place - including Japan. But getting a proper steer from the blokes in suits who really called the shots in the CFF wasn't easy. She said the Federation's left hand didn't always know what its right was doing. Or something to that effect anyway: I think she may have used the words 'nunshoot', 'nunnery' and 'organise' somewhere. The one thing that had made her job a little easier was the fact that not many Belgians were expected to make the trip. She put this down to 9/11, which had taken place less than a month earlier; although quite why even al-Qaeda fanatics would see Belgian football fans heading for Croatia as any kind of a target neither she nor I could understand.

'Are you going to the game yourself?' I asked.

'Yes, but only because I have to,' she said. 'I must go to sit behind my boss,' she added in a resigned way. 'My lady boss. I don't really like football.' This seemed a bit of an odd thing to admit, but in Croatian terms the job probably paid well enough to be worth hanging on to.

Josip came from Split, and he was a fanatical Hajduk fan. Like a majority of the country's real fans, he was scornful of Dinamo Zagreb, Croatia's leading club in terms of recent success on the field, because of all the political and financial favours they had received. 'Dinamo are political club,' he said with utter distaste, 'but I'm a sports fan.' Allegedly, these favours included help from referees in games Dinamo (or Croatia Zagreb, as the late and not very lamented Croatian President Franjo Tudjman had insisted on renaming them) weren't even playing in - Rijeka would have won the Croatian championship in spring 1999, had a perfectly good goal not been disallowed for offside. Entirely coincidentally,

DINAMO ARE POLITICAL CLUB

Croatia/Dinamo won their simultaneous game to pip Rijeka for the title. Cynicism is, unsurprisingly, now widespread. It was all a far cry from the 1970s, in Tito's Yugoslavia, when Dinamo Zagreb could count on the support of virtually every Croatian for games against the big Serbian clubs - Partizan Belgrade or Red Star. All that is now in the past. Josip hadn't even supported Croatia Zagreb against foreign clubs in their only Champions' League campaign so far.

For all his disdain of football politics, Josip was another walking East European encyclopedia of football, even including Dinamo Zagreb stats. 'It was 0-0 with United at Old Trafford,' he said of Dinamo's Champions' League match-up with Sir Alex Ferguson's team a few seasons previously, 'and then United won here 2-1.' How many United fans would remember that, four or five seasons on?

Josip wouldn't take any money for the ticket.

Maybe it was the weather - 70 degrees, perfect sunshine - but central Zagreb is a relaxing place to wait around for a few hours. It isn't hard to find one of the two or three pedestrianised streets, running north from the main square in the old town, that are lined with pavement cafes for hundreds of yards up both sides, and once I'd found them, I didn't move for the rest of the morning.

By lunchtime, the main square was beginning to fill up with both Croatian and Belgian fans, but there was no trouble, despite the evident nationalism of the locals. A red and white checkerboard replica team shirt was more or less obligatory for the Croatian fans, as was a full repertoire of songs and salutes. The Belgians just let them get on with it, walking up and down wearing those velvety Viking helmets and carrying inflatable rubber tridents over their shoulders, as befitted their status as Les Diables Rouges, or Red Devils. 'We love you, Belgium, we do, oh Belgium, we love you' remained a favourite song, just as it had been at the San Marino game in Brussels back in February, and they still managed not to look embarrassed about it. A few of them came up to the cafes around me for a drink or two, alongside Croats doing the same. Everything was perfectly good-natured. Which is of course all as it should be; it was just so refreshing to see it come about so naturally, even before a game of this consequence. (During the World Cup itself, however, things weren't so friendly: a big screen transmission, in the same square, of Croatia's game with Italy ended up with people intimidated and hospitalised - and there wasn't really anyone there who could be perceived as an 'enemy'. At least no one was killed, unlike when Russian hooligans did the same thing after their game with Japan.)

Around 5pm I met Josip near the Maksimir Stadium. Before we went in, he insisted I change into a Croatian team shirt he'd brought along for me, in the design for Euro '96, and after the game he insisted I keep it. The stadium was obviously very new - so new in fact that it hadn't quite been completed yet. Today's capacity would be a little over 40,000, and it was set to rise to nearly 60,000 when the structure was finally ready, a venture which would include taking out the running track, lowering the level of the pitch and installing another 16,000 seats up close to the action.. Josip explained that Franjo Tudjman had decreed that his newly-independent country required a major new stadium, as befitted a country that had just come third in the World Cup. Huge amounts of money were sunk into the project, a project that had more than a whiff of hubris about it. Surely only a megalomaniac would give the country's name to his favourite club side. The stadium was not only to be a national one, but would remain home to Tudjman's beloved Dinamo/Croatia Zagreb.

Unfortunately for the by now ailing Franjo, the so-called Bad Blue Boys - the hardcore, semi-hooligan Dinamo/Croatia Zagreb fans, who took their name from the 1985 Sean Penn movie 'Bad Boys' - had become severely dischuffed at the way their team had been hijacked to become little more than a vehicle for the cult of Tudjman's personality. Political (and referees') favour may have brought success on the pitch, but to the BBB this success had come at too high a price - the spirit of the club. At the ceremonial opening of the Maksimir stadium North Stand in March 1999, the Bad Blue Boys created more than just a bit of a rumpus, in the course of which several running battles broke out and most of the brand new seating area was destroyed. As Tudjman himself looked on, the police apparently intervened in traditional uncompromising Balkan style and those several dozen Bad Blue Boys, who were generally deemed most successful at living up to their name were hauled off for an early appearance in front of Zagreb's chief beak.

Tudjman popping his clogs a year or so later was perfectly OK with Josip. He was fed up with the way that era's footballing mismanagement and corruption had dragged his country's status down both at home and abroad, just as it had reached the heights of France '98. The mismanagement had resulted in a drain of footballing talent to the West, a trend hardly unique in former Eastern Bloc countries, but particularly notable in Croatia. They may have been third in the World Cup, but domestic league attendances rarely top 2,000. He was proud that six of Croatia's Under-21 squad played for his home club Hajduk, but knew that they would leave Croatian club football as soon as they'd made any kind of name for themselves. In 2003 Dinamo's Nico Kranjcar, at the age of 19, is the latest bright Croatian footballing talent who looks set to do just that.

Even though we'd left ourselves plenty of time, it was touch and go whether we'd get in for the kick-off. CFF administration looked to be living well down to Vlatka's estimation when it turned out that only one small entry gate was open for the whole of the East Stand. The crush to get in was by far the worst I saw anywhere - or at least until I got to Kiev a month later. The gate was at the top of a flight of 15 concrete steps, and the barriers either side of it were 10 feet high, unclimbable by design, and would have been impossible to open or remove swiftly if things had got really dangerous. By the time people were getting through they were less than inclined to have their tickets checked or their pockets searched for weapons, alcohol or other nasties and so they were just steaming through on the way to their seats.

At least the CFF had managed to distribute the by-now standard freebie souvenir, which was waiting on each seat. This time it consisted of what looked like a hotel laundry bag which you put your hands in and held up to show the red and white Croatian flag printed on one side. The words to the Croatian national anthem were printed on the other side. To make sure you held this bag up the right way, it was helpfully marked with 'left hand' and 'right hand' in the designated corners. To remove any possible trace of doubt, there was a picture of an appropriately thumbed hand in both the corners in question. With user instructions like this, not even the dimmest Bad Blue Boy could fail to do what was required.

40,000 people were busy turning a physically ugly stadium into a psychologically intimidating one as well. The pitch of the stands was very steep, much like PSV's stadium in Eindhoven, which is jammed in between other buildings in a heavily developed urban area. This made the players appear, and possibly feel, very small. The whole North Stand here at the Maksimir was on its feet, brandishing its laundry bags, nearly all of which were being operated correctly, thus creating the desired wall of red and white. Just to make the wall complete, people were standing on the steps and in the gangways as well, and to hell with the safety risk. No one was in the right seat, because all the seats had had their number tag snapped off years ago, and there were no other indications anywhere either of what row you were on or what number seat you were looking at. Call me a soft, risk-averse Westerner, but this kind of thing can make a difference if you want to reduce the chances, or the severity, of an accident.

Josip was getting edgy. He didn't think Jozic, the Croatian coach, had made the right selection for a match Croatia had to win. In particular, why had he picked no fewer than six defenders in his starting line-up? Admittedly, some of these defenders were players of high quality and would have featured in many national line-ups, not least the no.5, Tudor, who played for Juventus. 'He has scored nine goals for Juventus,' Josip revealed. 'He's always in the right place at the right time.' Josip admitted to being a Juve fan, as well as supporting his beloved Hajduk. I'd noticed this kind of thing several times in former Communist countries - if a country's top players move overseas, the locals support the Spanish, English or Italian teams they move to, and largely give up on their own domestic football: AC Milan, for example, have a sizeable fanbase in Ukraine and Georgia on the strength of this. But Josip was too much of a fanatic to forget about Hajduk.

DINAMO ARE POLITICAL CLUB

Including substitutes who came on, today's Croatian line up featured no fewer than eight survivors from the France '98 squad, which was old enough by normal standards even then. Marko in Belgrade, who I'd heard get steamed up about the age of the Serbian squad, would only have had to come to Zagreb to see that the Croatian squad could match the Serbs zimmer-frame for zimmer-frame. If Croatian TV had wanted to do a remake of Dad's Army (and you never know - the original On The Buses reached number one in 1970s Yugoslavia, and Norman Wisdom is 'big in Albania', so there's no accounting for cultural taste in the region), this squad could have gone straight into the recording studio after the game. Stanic, Jarni, Soldo, Vlaovic, Simic, Tudor, Suker and Prosinecki were all there tonight, as was Alen Boksic, due to be tonight's hero, and like the others in the autumn of his footballing years. Suker had no club affiliation at the time and was therefore unlikely to be 100% match fit, and how many of the others still had the legs we were about to find out. It was as if Sven-Goran Eriksson had wheeled out David Seaman for England's vital home Euro 2004 qualifier against Macedonia. The very idea would be laughable.

Josip reckoned that if Croatia qualified for Korea/Japan, this Home Guard of Zagreb-on-Sea would either want, or be pressed, to carry on until June before finally hanging up their polyester shirts and shin pads. Before coming here, I'd talked about the advanced age of Croatia's first choice team with Igor, who lived in Rijeka, near the Adriatic coast. Igor reckoned that although Jozic had begun the process of introducing a younger generation of players, the process wouldn't be complete in time for the following year's World Cup finals. Prosinecki was OK still, Igor thought, for a game played at a measured pace, and his reading of the game and timing of a pass were still tip-top. 'But year are year,' he concluded tellingly.

When everyone put their laundry bags down after the anthem, Josip spotted his elder brother and nephew a few seats along in the row in front of us, even though neither they nor we were in our allotted seats. His nephew was 14 years old but already over six feet tall with shoulders to match, so I was glad I wasn't standing behind him. The game kicked off, and as the minutes went by with the score still 0-0, Josip began to fret more and more about the number of underemployed Croatian defenders on the field. There were midfield and striking options on the bench, but coach Jozic didn't see any need to bring them on.

After half an hour I went off to get some drinks from a bar under the stand. Leaving your seat is usually a good way of making things happen, and sure enough there were two huge roars while I wasn't able to watch - one when a penalty was awarded to Croatia for a push in the box, and another when Prosinecki hoofed it over the bar and into Row Z, Beckham in Istanbul-style. Half-time arrived, still goalless.

Against a background of Croatian pop music over the PA, Josip told me a bit more about himself. It was as if he wanted to get things off his chest, or to explain to an outsider how things had been in his country in recent troubled years. Seeing it as his duty to enlist, he had fought in the Bosnian wars of 1993 to 1995, taking part in some of the successful Croatian campaigns of the time. He'd seen six months of active service, in which time he'd been able to have a shower twice.

One morning, from his firing position high on a hillside, he'd seen a UN vehicle - attached to the UNPROFOR mission - in the valley below him. The UNPROFOR troops locally were Russian and, rightly or wrongly, the Croats suspected that their neutrality might not have been total; in other words that the Russians were backing their co-religionists, the Orthodox Serbs, against the Catholic Croatians. Josip didn't tell me exactly what he had seen, but he became convinced that the Russians in the vehicle were indeed running arms and ammunition to local Serbian units. He waited until the vehicle was empty and then opened fire on it. The vehicle burst into flames and then blew up. His Croatian commanders took a dim view of this, reckoning that even if the Russians were supplying guns to the Serbs in breach of UN neutrality, destroying UN vehicles with automatic gunfire was hardly upholding the Croatian side of the non-combatants bargain. For this, Josip was held in jail for a month by his own side.

Not unnaturally, the whole experience of a shooting war had scarred him. He stopped short of describing everything he'd witnessed, but he had evidently seen or come to hear of tragic events. I didn't press him: it was a new and uneasy experience for me too to talk to someone so closely and recently involved in violent conflict. 'Many war crimes,' he said quietly, and then gestured to the thousands of people around him, as if to show he wasn't alone and to highlight how deeply Croatian society had been involved in, and even implicated in, the struggle. Thousands of those here tonight could probably have recounted similar stories. There is a memorial behind the West Stand of the Maksimir stadium to the many Dinamo 'Bad Blue Boys' who lost their lives in this conflict.

Half-time snacks consisted of donuts, roast chestnuts and the obligatory sunflower seeds: clearly England is about the only country where you can watch football without being forced to consume enormous quantities of birdseed. The crowd were getting edgy, which wasn't surprising, given that Croatia were 45 minutes from facing a play-off somewhere as yet unknown.

Belgium were clearly playing for the goalless draw that would see them through automatically. As often happens, this conservative, run-the-clock-down approach would turn out to be their downfall, only not yet. The second half wore on and Croatia still didn't have the goal they desperately needed. Their agitation began to show on the field, with more aggressive tackles going in and more ambitious passes being attempted. Jozic at last responded to his side's dire need for a goal by bringing on some more attacking players. Only 13 minutes were left when a cool-headed Alen Boksic tapped on a short-range shot for what looked like the crucial score. 'Boksic, Boksic, Alen, Alen Boksic' chanted the crowd throughout those remaining 13 minutes. At once the nature of the game altered - now it was Croatia who had what they needed, and they were the ones sitting back to protect it. But it was dicey because they were doing so with midfielders and strikers, having taken most of their defenders off. With six defenders in his starting line-up, Jozic was unlikely to have included much top defensive talent among the substitutes. Belgium came close, very close, to pulling the goal back, but the local side held on to win.

Cue wild celebrations in the stands, on the pitch and in the streets after the final whistle. Josip believed this 1-0 win, unremarkable purely as a game of football, was the most important sporting event for his country since France three years before, even outranking Ivanisevic's fairy-tale Wimbledon win (at tennis, not in Milton Keynes) the previous July. He'd arranged to meet Vlatka, freed from her official duties, at the tram stop round the back of the stadium and we walked back towards the city centre. Cars raced by, trailing flags, and horns blared constantly, even on cars heading towards the stadium whose drivers presumably couldn't have been at the game. Even Vlatka, the non-fan, was impressed that her 'small country' would be present at the finals of a major global event.

We chose a café with a pavement terrace on the main road into the city. I asked Vlatka if she knew the England-Greece result, and she rang her brother to find out, which is how I first heard about that last-minute Beckham free kick.

I was still wearing my Croatia shirt. Happy, but total, strangers waved to me on their way by and came up to shake my hand. Eventually I decided I should be honest, and told one group that I was English. 'Very good,' they said. 'Shering-ham. Totting-ham.' These guys were from the Ossie Ardiles school of English. Croatia Zagreb's coach for the 1999-2000 season? Step forward one Ossie Ardiles. Zagreb comes in marginally ahead of another one of Ossie's clubs, Swindon Town, in the glamour stakes, I suppose; but in Josip's opinion, Ardiles was 'a funny guy', and no one at the club really took him seriously, even at an Alice-in-Wonderland outfit like Tudjman's Croatia Zagreb.

Vlatka had to get back to her mother's flat in the west of the city and needed a tram from the main square, so we set off again. She'd be back at work on Monday helping to administer two Croatian women's internationals; and a November tour to Korea for the men looked on the cards, now that Croatia were safely through to the World Cup. Even though she wouldn't get to go there herself, the tour was still good news because the pressure of work would be off during the tour, with so many CFF bigwigs away 'fact finding' in top hotels on the other side of the world. It wasn't the greatest job, as she wasn't that much of a fan, but she valued it because opportunities were otherwise so limited, even for someone with good English. After the civil war, an influx of 'ethnically-cleansed' Bosnian Croats into Croatia itself had exacerbated existing economic difficulties, for all the apparent affluence on display in the city centre. 'There are no jobs, no money, no opportunity,' said Josip, who lived 20 kilometres from the centre, and for whom even the tram fare into Zagreb was a problem.

We said goodbye at a tram stop in the centre. In the months that followed, a chance arose for me to repay the kindness Josip and Vlatka showed me by helping them as they had spontaneously helped me, but they insisted that they didn't want me to do anything of the kind. Croatia has had a bad press in the last decade (although nothing like as much as Serbia), but individuals everywhere can give the lie to that.

That day's round of matches was the last in the qualifiers proper, although eight European teams who had come second in their respective groups would now play off in pairs for one of four further UEFA qualifying places for Korea/Japan. Belgium were one of these eight teams, and tonight they had joined Hungary and Romania in the list of countries it had been my not exactly unalloyed pleasure to see play twice. Les Diables Rouges headed disconsolately for home. The draw for the play-offs set them up for a home and away tie with the Czech Republic, who'd lost out to Denmark in the race to finish top of Group Three.

Belgium won it, and knocked the Czechs out of the tournament. This went relatively unnoticed, so surprised was everyone that the Netherlands had come only third out of the three main contenders in their qualifying group, by failing to register a win in either game against Ireland. The Republic's reward for coming second was a fun-packed trip to Iran, from which the winners would pass Go on their way to Korea or Japan. Football isn't all about Tuesday evenings away to Mansfield in the Nationwide.

YOU COME WITH ME - I GET TICKETS

In the other play-offs, Slovenia were to take on Romania, while Turkey would have to wait a while to see if they would be taking on Austria or Israel. In view of the September 11 attacks and the greatly increased volatility of the situation in the Middle East, the Austrians had been unwilling to travel to Tel Aviv as scheduled on this final weekend of qualifying games. UEFA backed them, and the game had been rescheduled for October 27; still three weeks away, and still in Tel Aviv.

Thanks to Vlatka's brother, I knew that David Beckham's last-throw-of-the-dice Old Trafford free kick had secured England the point they needed to condemn Germany to a play-off, which turned out to be against Ukraine. Taking on Rebrov and Shevchenko in their own Kiev backyard in mid-November would be no easy task for Rudi Voeller's side. The Turkey/Austria/Israel grouping would feature two teams I hadn't already seen play, so I aimed to get into the Istanbul leg of that one on November 14; but for now, the Kiev game on November 10 looked like the one for me.

15.

I am Doctor Zoom

**Ukraine - Germany, NSK Olympic Stadium, Kiev,
Saturday 10 November 2001**

I'D HAVE GIVEN a lot of Euros to know what was going
through the minds of the German squad as they walked off their
chartered aircraft in Kiev. Thanks to fouling up completely
against England in Munich, here they were buttoning up their
sponsored suits against the wind and rain of another East
European early winter, instead of settling back to enjoy a
leisurely run-out against Thailand in Bangkok. As every English
football fan discovered, but will never tire of being reminded,
the German FA, assuming that their boys would come top of
their group, had arranged an acclimatising, mini Far-Eastern tour
for their team, to take place on the international match dates in
November. Unfortunately for them, they hadn't yet won their
qualifying group. So when Beckham's Old Trafford free-kick
went into the top corner of the Greek net, the first thing the
German FA had to do was cancel all their plans and rush off to
the travel agent and enquire about the availability of a couple of
dozen seats on flights to Ukraine instead. Or while they're about
it, maybe a whole charter aircraft.

It was a winner-takes-all, two-leg play-off. Would the Germans
be psychologically up for it? That 5-1 hammering in September
must have cut pretty deep. Ukraine were an unpredictable awkward
squad, with a couple of world-class players in Shevchenko and
Rebrov, veterans of the successful 1999 Dinamo Kiev side. This
was Ukraine's best opportunity ever to break through to the World
Cup Finals themselves, and they'd be going for it alright.

YOU COME WITH ME - I GET TICKETS

But sadly for supporters of the underdog everywhere, if any footballing country could handle this kind of thing mentally, you'd put your house on it being the Germans. France? On their day, possibly. Spain? Never. England? Too fragile, too unused to delivering when it really counts, whatever the sport, at least until Jonny Wilkinson came along. One country to play a game to save your life? Germany every time.

You could hardly say that Rudi Voller (or Rudi Feller, as his name came out in translation) was put under the microscope at the first press conference. If Sven-Goran thought that Italian journalists were no more than 'kindergarten' standard compared to British ones armed with the Ulrika Jonsson story, then East European ones are barely out of nappies. Most of their questions smacked of desperation, of inferiority, of a deep desire to be taken seriously by the mighty 'Bundesteam'. 'But don't you fear Shevchenko?' the man from the sports paper *Komanda* asked pleadingly. 'We'll work something out,' said Feller helpfully. And when a Ukrainian journalist finally plucked up the courage to ask for Feller's take on recent German footballing misfortunes, his reply was simply, 'Why talk about that now?' And that was that. No follow-up, end of debate.

For me, the Ukraine-Germany pairing had looked easily the pick of the five play-offs, unless you fancied a trip to Tehran with Mick McCarthy's Ireland. Which, I have to say, I did. Seeing a game under the gaze of the Ayatollahs and 120,000 fans would have been something to talk about in the pub back at home (as, let's face it, you wouldn't have been able to talk about it in the snug bar of the Hen and Chickens in downtown Tehran). But when I had to make my plans, it wasn't clear which Asian country would be Ireland's opponents. For a while it looked like being Kazakhstan, or one of the other Rug Belt, central Asian 'Tragicstan' countries. By the time Ireland's opponents were known to be Iran, I'd got my Ukrainian visa ($55 for a two-night stay in the country, thanks chaps).

My standard trawl through the footballing websites of the country I was going to took me to a chatroom on the Dinamo Kiev site, where the most opinionated contributions came from someone called Doctor Zoom. Here was a suitably off-the-wall contact, I thought, and vaguely English language-capable into the bargain. Maybe he could fix a ticket for me. I'd been round these houses often enough now to know I could pick up a ticket for not many dollars (about 10% of what the visa cost, probably) outside the ground, but I wanted to meet some genuine local fans, while preferably avoiding any genuine local policemen.

'Hello Endy!' said the e-mail I got back a few days later. Did he mean me? I think he did. 'I am Doctor Zoom. I am 20 years old. How old are you? In which city do you live?' His real name turned out to be Aleksandr, which sounded a bit prosaic, especially when you add in his two mates, Andrey and Sergey, who were going to the game too. They would sort me out. Sergey was a 'fun of Chelsea', unlike Doctor Zoom himself, who was an AC Milan fun. Andrey, almost uniquely outside the UK, turned out to be a Manchester United fun. He had equipped himself with a United scarf, a trophy from a school trip to the UK in 1996, and had also been to the Czech Republic, Austria and Sweden, so he was pretty widely travelled by Ukrainian standards. All of them thought Glenn Hoddle should have been playing Sergei Rebrov in Spurs' starting line-up every week, although the fact that Rebrov is Ukrainian may have caused them to overlook the fact that his performances in the Premiership to date had been characterised by the apparent use of two left feet, one of them pointing backwards.

'Do you like Obolon beer?' they asked a few days before I left. Well, there wasn't too much of it on sale at my local offie, that was for sure. 'We will regail you!!' I had to look up 'regail' in the dictionary. I didn't find it, but I think I knew what they meant.

Next day they mailed me a map of the stadium, with an X to mark the spot where our seats were. Getting from A anything like directly to B would turn out not to be these lads' strong suit, and despite their admission later that they had in fact marked the seats in the wrong block, in hindsight their map was possibly the most geographically accurate thing they did for me, in that it at least related to the right match in the right stadium. Thanks entirely to Doctor Zoom and his two bunglingly incompetent assistants, by the end of my weekend in Kiev I would be handing over cash dollars under the eyes of the local police, not for a match ticket, but as a backhander direct to an on-duty officer of the Kiev Constabulary for an emergency ride in a squad car to get me to the airport before the gate closed for my flight home.

Queueing at immigration on landing in Kiev, I saw Sven, the heavy-metalling Eintracht Frankfurt fan I'd met in Athens, in the next line. He looked a bit blank to begin with, but placed me in the end, or pretended to at any rate. Clearly neither his wife nor his pal Buffo, the heavy metal journalist, had fancied the Kiev trip that much, despite Ukrainian enthusiasm for metal music. Sven said he thought his party were in the Hotel Rus. He gave me his mobile number and we said we'd try to meet up.

'This is Fan Dee,' said Sergey on the concourse outside. Sergey, Andrey and Aleksandr, aka Doctor Zoom, had braved the weather to come out to meet me off the plane. Andrey was ostentatiously loading my luggage - all one of my bags, weighing about the same as a new baby - into the large and otherwise empty boot of an old Audi 100. Fan Dee was the driver and a friend of theirs, and very welcome the ride into town was. Fan Dee looked as if he was from the Russian Far East, despite the very English-looking tweed jacket he was wearing.

I asked whether Fan Dee came from Kamchatka, or somewhere like that.

'No, he is not Russian person,' said Sergey. 'He is from Vietnam.'

'What does he do? Is he a student as well, like you guys?'

'No, he is not student. He is worker.' Which seemed a bit of a put down, but FD's English didn't seem tip-top, so he couldn't argue the toss.

Fan Dee drove on silently while the rest of us talked about Ukrainian football, which basically meant Dinamo Kiev and the national side. Sergey's English was the best and the others looked to him when they hit a linguistic brick wall in what they wanted to say. After giving me my ticket for tomorrow, he reminded me that, for a while in the 1990s, Kiev supplied nine or ten of the Ukraine team. Nowadays it's only three or four. Dinamo Kiev had dropped their goalkeeper, Filimonov, after momumentally feeble Champions' League performances against both Liverpool and Boavista - the poor lad ended up later that season playing for Uralan, somewhere off in the Ural mountains about two days' train ride from Moscow. That would probably learn him not to flap so uselessly at crosses any more. Sholkhovskiy was now the man between the sticks.

Ukrainian football hasn't been helped by the break up of the USSR. Dinamo Kiev are clearly top dog domestically, and the lack of competition provided by other clubs means that Dinamo can't easily maintain the skill levels required to mount a credible campaign in the Champions' League. Shakhtar Donetsk, in the mainly Russian-speaking, industrial east of the country, also qualified for the Champions' League in 2000-01. They didn't shine, exactly, but they remain the toughest opposition Dinamo face at home. Apart from Donetsk-Kiev games, however, there isn't much for locals to get excited about in the domestic game, yet Premier League attendances average a respectable 10,000. In Soviet times, Dinamo Kiev-Spartak Moscow games were often marred by violence, and the possibility of trouble remains, given Spartak's current reputation. These days, the two teams scarcely ever meet.

After the 1999 season Dinamo had to, or chose to, break up a successful side and sold their best players - Rebrov, Shevchenko and others - for large sums to Western clubs. Shevchenko had to be sold in summer 1999, as he would have been out of contract with Kiev in 2000, and could then have left for free. Since 1999, Kiev's Champions League performances have fallen away.

Today's management at Dinamo are a different breed from the bunch in charge in the early 1990s, condemned as 'shiftless' even in the club's own, glossy, 70th anniversary brochure, published in 1997. In the 1990s, questions were asked about where the money from earlier player sales went to. Nowadays, things are different. According to Doctor Zoom, the 20 million dollars for Shevchenko had been invested in a training academy designed to identify and bring on the next Rebrovs and Shevchenkos. The academy, at Koncha Zaspa, about 30 miles outside the city, is starting to deliver the goods, and in the meantime quality talent has been bought, like Chernat, Peev, as well as Gioane from Romania, Idahor from Nigeria, and Shatskikh from Uzbekistan, of all places. Another couple of years and Dinamo may be a force in Europe once again.

As for tomorrow's World Cup game, Ukrainian superstar Andriy Shevchenko was doubtful with a broken nose, sustained playing for AC Milan against Bologna. It must be a nightmare for international coaches, they just can't get the players back fit when they return from a spell of club duty.

The Germans were in the same kind of boat. Oliver Kahn had picked up an injury in training with Bayern 10 days previously, but it looked as if he'd be fit, and he'd arrived with the rest of the team the day before. Rudi Voeller's German line-up, boldly announced over 48 hours before the game, featured five out-and-out defenders in front of Kahn's goal. No prizes for guessing that the 'Bundesteam' had come here to grind out a 0-0 and then finish the job in Dortmund the following week.

We were rolling through the suburbs now, and Andrey was determined to downwardly manage any expectations I might have of his home city. 'Chernobyl is our export,' he lamented. The politicians were all dishonest. Kiev was founded in the ninth century, 400 years before Moscow, he went on, but now only the centre of the city was brightly lit. I'd have called that a non-sequitur myself, but I let it go. There were gangland gunfights, carjackings, and mafia shootouts, almost as bad as in Moscow. Crime was rife and you had to pay all manner of backhanders just to start a business. And even that wasn't the worst of it, he said. Ukraine were highly unlikely to win tomorrow's game, that was the worst of it.

We crossed the huge Dnieper river, a mile wide at that point, but once on the right bank of the river, where most of the city lies, it became clear they hadn't the faintest idea where my hotel was. They did point out the leader of the Ukrainian Nationalist Party getting into a Honda and driving away, but the hotel he'd come out of was the wrong one, so it wasn't that big a help. Fan Dee was clearly just hoping for the best, or was at least hoping that these three native Kievites, with nothing at all to go on except the correct city centre street address that I'd sent them ten whole days ago, would somehow locate the right one of the half dozen or so big downtown hotels. I had a street map in my bag in the boot but, possibly on a point of pride, they wouldn't let me get at it. Then Andrey gave up, told Fan Dee to stop the car on the main street, and got out to ask the way.

He clambered back in and we turned round to go back the way we'd come, and Andrey resumed his Eeyore-like account of that week's blood-soaked drive-by mafia shootings. But we still weren't on the right road, so Andrey had to get out and ask again a few minutes later. Fan Dee was pulling off again when a large black car swerved right across his bumper, deliberately carving us up and jamming us into the kerb. Fan Dee steered right to try to get round the nose of the other car, but its driver moved forward again to stop us, blocking not only our car but at least two other lanes of traffic. Out the passenger door climbed a big man wearing a regulation black leather jacket and clutching an equally obligatory mobile phone in his hand. He walked slowly round to the door where Andrey had just climbed back in. Andrey wasn't looking too happy right now.

'You dropped your hat,' the man in the jacket pointed out helpfully.

After that we used the floodlights of the Olympic Stadium as a homing beacon, as the hotel I was in was just alongside it. In Kiev terms, 'alongside' meant almost a mile away, but it was a help of some sort. One of the teams must have been having a training session on the ground, as the lights were fully on, and my four friends managed to find the hotel from there.

It felt like, and in fact it was, a 1970s time capsule. Here, surviving against the free market odds, was a hotel that made no concessions to taste or style whatsoever. The predominant colour of everything was what the couple we bought our house from last year chose to call 'chocolate' brown, and everything had the unmistakable aura of Intourist, the one and only travel agency in Soviet times. The door, carpet, chairs, table, curtains, flock wallpaper and heavy velvet bedspreads in my room were all brown, as were the lampshades, the wall-mounted radio, the décor and fittings in the bathroom, and even, as a final touch, the water itself. The pillowcases were at least white, but made of a coarse material that would cause any self-respecting UK prison inmate to start a riot over conditions. And the Intourist name and logo were sewn into each one, in case anyone was tempted to nick one as a memento.

Next day I spent time taking in some of the sights, which Kiev undoubtedly has plenty of, including the amazing caves and underground passageways in the Kiev-Pechersky Monastery (or 'Historical-Cultural Monument', as the Soviets called it), where I'd arranged to meet Andrey and Aleksandr - Doctor Zoom. The tunnels are hundreds of yards long, threaten severe damage to the skulls of anyone above five feet tall; they are overheated, only partly lit, very crowded, and full of people carrying naked candle flames, since the whole point about the caves is that you go there to venerate the bones and mummified bodies of Orthodox saints and holy men. In the UK they'd only let you down into such a place with a miner's helmet on, and in a group of about three people. But health and safety is not the priority in Ukraine that it is in the UK, so experiences like this are still raw, vivid and real.

We spent our time down there among the holy men and the tombs talking about the likely condition of Shevchenko's nose. Would he play? Would it deter him from heading the ball? Was he tall enough for his heading ability to be a factor anyway? Could the Ukraine manager, the veteran, ex-USSR and current Dinamo Kiev coach Valery Lobanovsky - sadly now deceased - take the risk of playing him? More or less ignoring the skulls surrounding the mummified, glass-encased, shrunken body of St Nepomuk of Novgorod, Andrey and I agreed Shevchenko wouldn't miss this game for anything. This was tantamount to a World Cup Final for Ukraine, and the pressure to play, both on and from the player, would be too much to withstand. So it proved.

After the caves, Andrey and Aleksandr treated me to a tour of some only just obsolete Soviet military hardware, including battle tanks, fun-packed ICBM launchers and MI-24 helicopter gunships, the ones that look like angry wasps. For a few hrivny - the local currency - you can climb into the cockpit of one of these. One or two captured WWII German tanks are on display as well, although these are painted all over with pink and yellow flowers, as if they'd just turned up uninvited at the 1970 Isle of Wight rock festival. The Soviet material is treated with more dignity, and is left as it was, in military green.

All afternoon we saw fans who had just arrived in Kiev for the game from all over Ukraine. Judging by their scarves, they came from cities like Dnepropetrovsk, Lvov, Odessa and Donetsk, places which hardly register on the radar screens of English or Western fans, but cities where enthusiasm for the game is probably just as great, merely lacking the money and the glitz. In amongst them were hordes of local Dinamo Kiev fans as well.

We met Sergey at the foot of the massive Rodina Mat' statue - a 'Socialist Realist' construction of a classically-robed female warrior, overlooking the Dnieper river, and brandishing a sword in the hand of her upstretched arm. Sergey had spent the day helping his mum move her furniture into a new flat, but had been given time off for the game. We set off back into town, but then Aleksandr spotted some more main battle tanks, short-range missiles and mini armoured submarines over to the left, in an area we hadn't been to yet. Clearly Doctor Zoom was a bit of an anorak for outdated lethal military equipment. 'Lots of technik,' he said enthusiastically, so we had to go over and take a look, posing for photos underneath what felt like an entire division's worth. Then finally we went for some food at a restaurant near the stadium.

As with fans everywhere I'd been since September, England's 5-1 win in Munich had gone down well here, although I still got the feeling from these three that they'd rather Ukraine were playing England in this play-off instead of Germany. Not because of the kudos attached to playing England - they just thought it more likely they would win. But even Andrey was in a sunnier mood today and confidently forecast a 2-0 win for his team.

These three Ukrainians had lived in Kiev all their lives. Yet they spoke Russian among themselves. I asked them why, and the answer appeared to be that it was what their parents spoke. They were a serious, cultured and conformist lot, earnestly pursuing their studies on the long road to a better life than their parents' generation had been able to enjoy. They asked me what books and music I liked, and then Aleksandr dropped the wacky, website Doctor Zoom persona completely and asked me which Italian film director I most admired. I could only hope the name I gave him actually was an Italian film director.

Ukrainian fans evidently aren't ones for getting to their seats early so as to enjoy a drink and a good sing for a couple of hours before the game, not when there's overcrowded, steamed-up buses to sit in, or gastrically very iffy hot dog stalls to hang out at near the metro station. At the place where we were, with under half an hour to go before the 7pm kick off, Andrey and the others all ordered a plate of chips each. Well aware that Ukrainians like to take their time preparing food, they sat back and chatted about art nouveau in early 20th Century Kiev architecture. I just watched the clock.

Ten minutes later Sergey, who had everybody's tickets except mine, which he'd given me in Fan Dee's car on the way in from the airport the day before, took a call on his mobile from his brother. Sergey had his brother's ticket as well, so he had to go and meet him at the metro station. Even he realised that unless he found his brother sharpish, he'd miss the kick-off, but instead of giving the others their tickets before leaving, he just waltzed off, leaving his share of chips to the others and mumbling something as if to say that he could be gone a while. When he didn't come back we had to try to find him, and his unknown brother, in the dark, among only 82,000 people, with fifteen minutes to go to kick-off in what was, after all, quite an important game.

Ukrainians are no different from anyone else when it comes to all looking the same at night. Andrey was beside himself with frustration, though whether at Sergey, or at himself for not thinking to get the tickets off his friend at the restaurant, I couldn't tell. Sergey's brother was probably still only halfway up the escalator. Given the swampy, river bed terrain on which the city lies, the Kiev metro is built extremely deep, so that at Arsenalnaya station (Arsenal - we could try calling a tube station that in London) it's a good six or seven minutes from the platform up to ground level.

At 6.55, with no sign of Sergey's brother, Andrey suggested I go and find my seat, which seemed a sensible move, as I at least had a ticket. In Moscow, there had been four levels of security and an X-ray to get through before you could get into your seat. Fortunately, here there was simply a gate for each block with an official standing there to check tickets. At 6.57 that evening, it's fair to say he was as busy as he was likely to be at any time that season, with three hundred people who'd left it to the last minute all pushed up against the metal bars and demanding admission now. Again, the health and safety people would have had a field day at this total free-for-all, in which if you weren't aged between 15 and 50, fairly strong, and probably male, you'd have a choice between probably being seriously injured or opting out of it and missing the first 20 minutes of the game. The pressure of people streaming into the ground was so great that he was quite unable to check anyone's ticket or even see that they had one. Unfortunately he couldn't therefore tell me that I was in fact in the wrong block, something which I didn't realise until after the game, and so I saw the whole game from a seat belonging to someone else, who never showed up. Even if Sergey had located his missing brother, they would now never locate me. I began to feel a bit more charitable about Doctor Zoom's navigational skills.

My seat, whoever's it really was, did have a great view, and I was just in time to mumble along with the Ukrainian national anthem, helpfully printed on the front page of the *Komanda* sports paper. Just about everyone had an air-horn, including a particularly annoying 13-year old lad a few seats along from me who never let up until half-time, when his mum had to step in and take it off him because everyone in earshot would have happily whacked him with it by that stage.

Andrey was looking like a half-decent pundit when, after 18 minutes, Ukraine went one up through a Zubov strike. But Michael Ballack, whom Liverpool, United and South Korean fans may well remember better than most, had levelled it at 1-1 before half-time. Shevchenko was playing, but he wasn't much of a threat. Maybe the most famously injured nose in Ukrainian football was playing a part after all by reducing its owner's effectiveness. The Germans were packing midfield and defence, and were severely restricting the Ukrainians for room. Meanwhile the German goal was a soft one, and when it went in there was a critical drop in the mood inside the stadium. It stayed at 1-1 until the end. Ukraine would have it all to do in Dortmund the following Wednesday, as these games were on 'European' lines: in other words, away goals counted 'double'. Now the Germans had an away goal in the bag, despite having packed their defence in the hope of a 0-0.

The home fans never let up their support. 'U - KRA - INA! U - KRA - INA!' everybody yelled. But in this open arena the noise simply vanished into the sky. 1-1 must have been a real disappointment to them, with the away leg still to come, in which the 'Bundesteam' surely would have the better prospects. Perhaps symbolically, the electronic stadium clock packed up halfway through the second half, once it became clear that this would not be the Ukrainians' night. But at no time did the locals turn against or jeer at their own team. Ukrainian President Leonid Kuchma was at the game, although the man on the PA didn't announce him, unlike with Moscow mayor Luzhkov back in June. Maybe Kuchma would have got all the jeers the crowd didn't give their underperforming national team, Ukrainian politics not being exactly squeaky clean.

At the end the players, and the crowd, all trooped away disconsolately. For all everyone's hopes of an upset, it had been a pretty standard, routine German performance, as workmanlike and predictable as a Michael Schumacher Formula 1 win. England's 5-1 in Munich had been Germany's first competitive defeat since Euro 2000, and would be their last until coming up against Ronaldo in the World Cup Final itself. By getting an away goal here in Kiev they did enough when it counted, and with solid defence they kept the home team to just one. To come back from Ukraine's opening goal, after the setbacks of the previous couple of months, said a lot for the character of the German side, even if it didn't have you dancing in the gangways with delight. To coin a phrase, it had been just like watching Germany.

I AM DOCTOR ZOOM

By ringing my room, Andrey, Aleksandr and Sergey met up with me after the game and we went for another round or two. They were philosophical, which probably meant that they expected the Germans to clean up in Dortmund - as indeed happened. Back home at the city's Westfalenstadion, where Germany hadn't lost for over a quarter of a century, Rudi Voeller's team put the tie beyond any doubt with three goals in the first 15 minutes, after what Andrey called the 'rudest' mistakes by the Ukrainian defence. Ukraine left Rebrov on the bench, while for Germany, Voller had restored Jancker and Neuville to the attack in place of Asamoah and Zickler. Neuville duly tucked away the second German goal in the return leg. Andrey told me later that he couldn't even blame the ref. He was so upset afterwards that he threw a sickie and didn't go into university lectures the following day, which for a studious lad like him was a pretty serious reaction.

Managerial vulnerability is by no means an exclusively English phenomenon. Valery Lobanovsky resigned as Ukraine coach after this game in Dortmund, with 1970s superstar Oleg Blokhin, possibly the most famous Dinamo Kiev player of all time, an early favourite to take over from him. In the end the job went to Leonid Buryak.

On Sunday morning the gates of the Olympic Stadium were open, so I went inside for a quick look in daylight. The Coca Cola-sponsored coffee tent was still standing, in a recess between two enormous concrete supports for the upper tier of seating, smothered with graffiti for something called the 'Crazy Legion' and Cyrillic letter 'D's - for Dinamo Kiev. Apart from that there was really very little to suggest that, arguably, the biggest game in Ukraine's history (at least until the following Wednesday) had been played there not more than 12 hours before.

My flight home was due off in mid-afternoon, which presented another challenge for my friends' navigational skills. Sergey was still helping his mum with her new flat, but Andrey and Doctor Zoom were free.

'Which way do you want to get to the airport?' they asked me, which wasn't a good start.

YOU COME WITH ME - I GET TICKETS

Fan Dee wasn't available today, perhaps assuming that, on Friday's showing, he was unlikely to be back much before nightfall. So we took the metro as far out of the city as we could, back over to the left bank of the Dnieper. There was a good chance that we could find a no. 316 bus here that would take us out to Kiev's Borispol airport.

'That one!' cried either Andrey or Doctor Zoom, I didn't notice who. It wasn't a 316, but it did say 'Borispol' in the front window, so we got on. It was a sunny afternoon, very warm for November, and we set off eastwards through the suburbs. This was clearly Andrey's part of town. Virtually every major building in this part of the city turned out to be either somewhere he had lived or was the workplace of one or other of his relatives. His dad was a doctor in that hospital, while his uncle was apparently a Director in that 'industrial complex' over there.

I had no idea where I was, as initially this wasn't the route Fan Dee had brought us in on Friday night, but when we passed the Kiev Hero City memorial, we were on the road to Borispol and I relaxed a bit.

I couldn't help noticing three things, however. Firstly, the goat tethered to the back seat didn't look as if it was about to catch a BA flight to Gatwick Airport in Sussex. Secondly, besides us, most of the other passengers on the bus were very small, although that was probably because they were mainly live chickens, carried on in big nets by two old ladies. I wondered whether the chickens would be cabin baggage or if they would have to go in the aircraft hold. I was still mulling over what this all might mean when I noticed the third thing, which was the bus shooting right past the turning for the airport. We were going to Borispol, for sure, but not Borispol airport; much like a bus to Luton won't necessarily take you to Luton airport. Borispol itself was a small town in its own right, and pleasant enough in the autumn sunshine, as I saw when we got off there a few minutes later, but it wasn't exactly where I wanted to be, with my flight due to depart in under two hours. I pointed this out to Andrey.

But Andrey was confident, on the outside at least. Trolleybus no. 2 would get us to the airport, no problem, he said, and a faded sign indicated that it would indeed stop right here, where we had got off the non-316 bus. Over the road, the police were making a bit of extra weekend cash by stopping motorists and then ripping them off on their way out of Kiev. There was time to watch them in action. Cars with nothing much apparently wrong mechanically, and which were being well-driven ('Is this fume-belching Kamaz truck being well-driven? Call Kiev 08705...') were being pulled over, and the driver made to get out and produce all sorts of papers which could then be found not to be in order.

Trolleybus no. 2 didn't come, and the time was ticking by. Maybe, I thought, for a few dollars, the police would like to give me a lift to the airport. I mentioned my plan to Andrey. After all, if you're lost and need to get somewhere, you ask a policeman, don't you? And they did have a squad car of their own, a top-of-the-range Soviet-era Zhiguli Fiat.

Fair play to him, Andrey went across the road and was soon deep in discussion with the local boys in grey-blue peaked caps. The one in charge nodded, finished fleecing the latest innocent driver to be stopped, got into his car, pulled across to our side of the road and fleeced me instead - a dollar a mile for the five miles to the airport. But time wasn't on my side and I couldn't think how else to get out of the position I was in. The cop told me that he was doing me a favour, and that Andrey had in fact beaten him down from twice his opening demand.

Even though I'd gained some early grey hairs as a result of Andrey's navigational skills, in Ukraine I'd once again met helpful locals I was indebted to, not just for sorting out a match ticket for me but also for the insights into their country and their genuine friendship. I told them that if they ever made plans to come to England, as they told me early the following year that they wanted to, they now knew where to find a friendly bobby who, for a consideration, would help take them to and from their home airport without having to negotiate either mobile phone-wielding guys in black cars, or babushkas with netfuls of live poultry.

16.

Number 10 is
Hagi Number

**Turkey - Austria, Ali Sami Yen Stadium, Istanbul,
Wednesday 14 November 2001**

EARLY IN THE 2001-02 English season, Roy Keane struck again, as he was later to do on a training pitch in the Far East with the first whistle of the World Cup only a referee's intake of breath away. Complaining about what he believed was a lack of atmosphere at Manchester United home games, compared with, say, Liverpool or Newcastle, he dismissed the many spectators at Old Trafford who were there on corporate hospitality jollies as 'prawn sandwich eaters'. Even some Manchester United fans were stung by the remark, given that there may possibly have been the odd grain of truth in it.

But my conscience felt fairly clear on this one, even as I took my seat on the VIP balcony in Galatasaray's Ali Sami Yen Stadium. So far, I'd seen 14 games and well over 20 different national teams, all of them by sitting, or more often standing, alongside local fans. I'd never failed to get in, and I'd never failed to meet plenty of ordinary people, ranging from taxi drivers, street cleaners, engineers, students and hacked-off officials to statisticians, electricians and war veterans. Iceland had been the only place I'd gone to where I'd met anyone else from Britain, at least to speak to; and I had been confident of making it a full set of games watched from the terraces by joining Galatasaray's famously phlegmatic, take-it-or-leave-it fans in the Ali Sami Yen

Stadium in Istanbul. Then the Turkish FA ruined everything by putting me in the VIP section with all the local chiefs and the suits from UEFA.

As I'd left it a bit late before sitting down at home and picking up the phone to the Turkish FA to ask for a ticket to the biggest game in their season, there wasn't time to post me the ticket I managed to get. Instead, the lady I spoke to said that as the ticket would be free, as a generous gesture from the Turkish FA, she would leave it for me at my hotel. Unfortunately I hadn't yet booked one, so that meant some more rapid phone calls to fix a hotel room, followed by another call to the Turkish FA telling them which hotel I'd like them to take my ticket to.

This all worked out beautifully, as they say, except that she didn't tell me it would be a VIP ticket. If I'd known, I might not have gone in my standard gear of T-shirt and not terribly smart trousers. But the Ali Sami Yen gatemen weren't like their MCC counterparts at Lord's. No one seemed in the least bit bothered about what I was wearing. They were far more bothered about whether I had any coins in my pockets, in case I decided to lob them gently or not so gently in the direction of the players. It was Turkey's most apologetic policeman (although that isn't saying very much, is it?) who searched me, but there was no way I was going to get in with the British loose change I'd been left with at Heathrow. At over two million lira to the pound, you only need 500 pounds to be a billionaire in Turkey, and it's a more or less exclusively banknote economy, so coins are virtually valueless and just right to throw onto the field. I had five pounds in coins and thus stood to lose a cool ten million. Evidently, VIPs couldn't be trusted any more than the rank and file fan not to throw the coins at the players. In the event, Austria's performance turned out to be so poor you'd never waste anything as valuable as a pound coin on them. Not like, say, Macedonia's; one of their players was struck by a coin from the Turkish crowd during the two countries' Euro 2004 qualifier, which sparked off a UEFA investigation and put Turkish fans in the dock with English ones.

Tonight's play-off second leg would decide whether Turkey or Austria qualified for the World Cup Finals, and Austria, a goal down from the home leg, were staring down the barrel. But they'd shown in Israel a fortnight before that they could pull off some surprises against the odds. Needing one more goal in Tel Aviv to finish second in their qualifying group, and thus to qualify for this play-off with Turkey (are you with me so far?) they left it until the 90th minute to score the goal that put the Israelis out. When the time came to pick a squad for the play-off with Turkey, they refused to pick any of the players who'd chosen to stay safely at home in Austria rather than chance things in Tel Aviv, which probably helped team spirit, but did nothing for their chances against a rapidly-improving Turkish team. I'm sure FIFA have nothing against the Israeli team, but their elimination at least avoided a major security nightmare not only tonight but at the World Cup Finals themselves.

Turkey's problems were different. They'd not qualified for the finals since 1954, so they had something of a 47-Year Itch to overcome. Public expectation was massive, and so were the expectations of the Turkish FA's Executive. 'Having targeted to play in the finals of the 2002 World Cup,' wrote Executive Committee Member Selami Ozdemir rather pompously in the match programme, 'we will do whatever is necessary to finalise our duty successfully.' The 'missed victories and successes' had to be attained, he said. Turkish coach Senol Gunes came over as a bit less driven, hoping merely for an 'honourable victory and beautiful football'. But there also was Gunes' problem - at the time. Football in Turkey is all about drive and passion: just ask the original 1993 'Welcome To Hell' Manchester United squad. Gunes, in the eyes of many fans, lacked sufficient sparkle, much as some English fans think Sven could usefully try and look a bit more annoyed sometimes. Before Turkey qualified, Gunes seemed at risk of losing his job to someone with a bit more pazzazz. After Turkey qualified, he could have turned up at the games fast asleep, and the fans would still have loved him.

I took a taxi into town, as I'd just missed the hourly bus from the airport. With the local currency the way it is, and the drivers the way they are, the meter in my taxi was mounting up quicker than the English goal tally had done in Munich a few months before. When this one reached 10 million, or eight digits, it just gave up, went back to zero and started again. So on really long journeys, the driver - or more likely the passenger - has to try to work out not only how often the mileometer's gone round the clock, but the meter as well.

To begin with I thought I'd got the only taxi driver in Istanbul with zero knowledge of football, but he did at least know that some of the Turkey squad (three of them at the time, later to be four when Hakan Unsal joined Blackburn) played their club football in the UK. He was much better at knowing which areas of Istanbul were best avoided, by day as well as by night. The Dolapdere district we were going through was 'famous', he said, for 'women, hashish and heroin - it's the only business'. I was staying less than half a mile away from there, near Taksim Park in the centre. The following April, a gang of Chechens held some Greek visitors hostage in a hotel a couple of streets away from the hotel I was in. And all this was of course long before the climate arose that gave rise to the two Istanbul suicide bombings in late 2003. Tonight, however, Turkey had celebration on its mind.

We were coming up to a modest 16 million lira for this ride when we got to the hotel. 16 million lira works out at about 13 dollars, the currency we'd agreed I would pay in. 'That'll be 30 dollars then please,' he said as he pulled up outside. If English isn't your first language, it's funny how easily 13 and 30 can get muddled.

You had to talk into an entryphone and climb up one floor on a broad spiral staircase before you got to the reception desk in this place. The Police's 'Roxanne' and the posh tones of the BBC World TV channel competed for the attention of anyone who might be listening. I turned the corner of the stairs to see the owner waving an envelope at me. On it was the distinctive crescent moon and star from the country's flag and at the bottom were all the Turkish FA sponsors' logos, local brands like Adidas, Mercedes and Pepsi. Inside it, more importantly, was a ticket for tonight's game, hand-delivered as promised by someone from the FA. Given that it contained a ticket for the posh stand, this amounted to pretty good service.

YOU COME WITH ME - I GET TICKETS

Turkish fans have a fearsome reputation, at least in England. But then you could argue that England fans have a pretty fearsome reputation, not only in Turkey but just about everywhere. Well before England's Euro 2004 qualifier there, our perception of Turkish fans had been shaped by one or two fairly recent and undeniably tragic incidents. Leeds played Galatasaray there a few seasons ago in a UEFA Cup semi-final, and two Leeds fans were stabbed to death. Hugely tightened security levels prevented any chance of 'reprisals' at the home leg at Elland Road a week or two later, but at the final in Copenhagen the following month, Arsenal and Galatasaray fans picked up from where things had left off in Istanbul. The Copenhagen episode seemed to be a six and two threes as to who 'started it' - you can rely on any thug from any country to say the other lot started it, like kids in a primary school playground. But what was often overlooked in all of this was that the Leeds visit was the first time Turkish fans had been involved in any hooliganism directed at foreign supporters, and until Copenhagen, there had never been any occurrence of Turkish fans causing trouble abroad. If only English fans could say the same. English sensitivities won't have been helped, however, by a Turkish court's decision in spring 2003 to release the killer in the Leeds assault, on the somewhat spurious grounds that he was goaded into it by Leeds fans. Murder is murder and should be treated as such, or so it universally seemed in this country. By the time of the two countries' Euro 2004 qualifier the following October, a real security headache was looming. Turkey were in UEFA's doghouse for the Macedonia coin-throwing incident only a few weeks earlier, but did UEFA show the vision to rap Turkish knuckles by making them play the England game behind closed doors, thereby greatly reducing the chances of trouble? Not likely - only travelling England fans lost out.

The hotel owner, Okan, spoke good English, and was a big time Galatasaray fan. The days when Romanian 'Maradona of the Carpathians' superstar Gheorghe Hagi played for the club were now long gone, but were fondly remembered by Okan. Nowadays, a majority of the club's squad is Turkish. Okan proudly told me that even though Galatasaray had sold nine players at the end of last season, this season they were an even better side. When the club gave one underperforming Brazilian his P45, they replaced him with four other players for the same money, and, for Okan, the obviously direct result of this dabbling in the Turkish transfer market was qualification for that season's Champions' League second Group stage. Two games with Liverpool were now on the cards. But Okan thought Michael Owen would cut them to pieces in those games.

The Turkey squad, he said, was built around Galatasaray, or former Galatasaray players, who knew each other and played for each other, and they would therefore play well in Japan. With hindsight, you have to hand it to Okan: not only did Turkey exceed everyone's expectations in the Far East, but they, and teams like Ireland and Senegal, showed what could be done at the very pinnacle of the game if you had a squad of relatively ordinary players who instinctively knew each other's game, as these Galatasaray players did. 12 of Turkey's 23 players for the finals were current, or former, Galatasaray players.

'Tonight, Turkey team play flowing football, you will see. The Austrians, they do only long ball over the top,' Okan went on. It sounded like the Austrian manager was Graham Taylor or Howard Wilkinson in disguise.

The stadium was at least three miles from the hotel, but I had lots of time to spare, so Okan drew me a map on the back of a dinner menu and I walked. On the arguably slightly flimsy evidence of walking across the city that evening, two years before the suicide bomb attacks of November 2003, I couldn't see much evidence of Turkey turning 'fundamentally' Muslim. Women wore trousers, talked on mobiles and drove cars, often all three simultaneously. There wasn't a beard in sight. Shops sold Hollywood blockbuster videos and lurid-looking local flicks as well. I passed an 'Oryantal Show', a 'Revu Show' and a 'Non-Stop Show' within a few hundred metres of each other, instantly bearing out what my taxi driver had said about Dolapdere. On the way back, some of their employees were standing on the pavements dressed in clothes that weren't really suitable for a November night, even in Turkey.

Maybe as sub-conscious self-defence from Dolapdere's more predatory residents, I stopped off for what turned out to be the most garlic-ridden sausage I've ever eaten. Up the road in Transylvania, vampires were updating their target maps and making plans to avoid me. As beer didn't seem to be an option, I ordered fresh orange juice as well, but it didn't appear on the bill. I pointed this out but the waiter waved a hand as if to say, forget it. I left a big tip.

The stadium is in an ugly part of town, overlooked by a concrete flyover, monstrously oversized advertising hoardings and grubby, off-white apartment blocks. It's quite small by international standards, holding only 33,000 or so, and most of it is open to the air, but there's plenty of noise when it's full. Roy Keane certainly wouldn't have anything to complain about if he was a Galatasaray player, though that's about as likely as, say, Turkey reaching the semi-finals of the World Cup itself, or Slovenia qualifying for the World Cup Finals rather than Holland. On the way in I bought a Besiktas Istanbul scarf. The stallholder pocketed my money, took a picture of me holding the scarf up, then took out his own Galatasaray scarf and kissed it.

Temporary food stalls offered kebabs, shashliks, deep-fried chicken, fresh vegetables, rice, couscous, freshly ground chilli, yoghurt, five types of bread, pretzels, and of course the obligatory sunflower seeds. It all smelt fantastic. The odds of contracting gastroenteritis or salmonella were maybe shorter than somewhere like Helsinki, but it was a world away from the anodyne hotdogs, coca-cola and chocolate bars you got in northern countries and it felt like a chance worth taking. Right alongside, in makeshift TV studios in gravel car parks, Turkish TV was interviewing former managers and players under bright lights, surrounded by eager youngsters. Despite the Besiktas scarf, people mistook me for an Austrian several times, but even though I was alone and seemed to be from a country that could deny these people entry to the World Cup Finals, I only encountered friendliness, which grew warmer after I told them I was English.

NUMBER 10 IS HAGI NUMBER

I went in, losing millions of lira on the way to the police anti-coin squad. My seat on the balcony was about level with the goal-line, but had the view of the game you'd expect from the VIP stand. I may have been English and underdressed, but no one seemed surprised to see me there. The floor was carpeted, the seats were cushioned, a free match programme had been laid out on each seat, and a bloke with a big bag came along the front throwing new Turkish squad T-shirts to anyone who wanted one.

In the next block were the 250 or so Austrian fans who had made the trip, with a detachment of police either side. Unlike the cop who'd searched me, these guys didn't look too apologetic about anything. Many wore the insignia of the Ozel Tim, the Interior Ministry police force, formed some years previously to take on the PKK insurgents. The PKK are Kurds, demanding independence and a Kurdish state in the south-east of the country (which would also take in a part of four other countries). But if you went with the official line, they're actually just rebellious Turks. Both sides' intransigence has been well documented.

Behind the goal and beyond the further detachment of police, were the first of the Turkish fans, who otherwise occupied every seat. All of them were singing and jumping up and down constantly. A brass band, all kitted out in red jackets and plumed helmets, marched up and down, trying not to look incongruous. 'Willkommen in der Hoelle' said a large banner behind the goal. Not very loosely translated, this meant 'Welcome to Hell' - the same cheery greeting the Galatasaray fans gave to the Manchester United team as they arrived for that Champions' League game in autumn 1993. The United team hotel was besieged by fans all that night, working on what amounted to a shift rota, in a bid to deny them any sleep. Whether the intimidation or attempted sleep-deprivation had any direct effect is impossible to tell, but United returned to Manchester empty-handed, so you could say it achieved what it set out to achieve. In English minds, the reputation of Turkish fans probably dates from that occasion. After all, in World Cup qualifiers in the 1980s, England had twice beaten Turkey 8-0, so there hadn't been all that much scope for demonisation before 1993.

YOU COME WITH ME - I GET TICKETS

Austria got predictable abuse when they came out for a warm-up, and this continued into the game whenever they had possession, which wasn't that often, to be truthful. Austria were woeful. With Toni Polster no longer in the squad, Andreas Herzog was about the only real quality player they had, as 23 international goals in 92 games just about underlines. But he couldn't carry the team on his own.

Nor could the Austrian fans. Singing 'There's Only One Thomas Winklhofer', for example, isn't much of a frightener to the opposition, who might be tempted to think that the Austrian team would actually be a bit stronger for there being just the one. 'Immer wieder, immer wieder Oesterreich' sang the 250 travelling hopefuls every now and again, whenever the locals shut up for a while, but they got drowned out more or less immediately by renewed Turkish chanting. Austria did create one good opening after 5 minutes, but that was it. After that, any attempt of theirs on goal went high over the bar, comically so at times. Turkey sat back and enjoyed the party, scoring after 21, 30, 44, 68 and 86 minutes for a 5-0 win on the night and 6-0 on aggregate.

Austria played so poorly that this had been on the cards more or less from the outset, which took something away from the game as a contest, but only 250 people in the whole ground cared about that. No doubt about it, the prawn sandwich eaters on the VIP balcony were right up with the ordinary fans when it came to celebrating the goals. Not until Galatasaray's Arif Erdem made it 5-0 did they sit back and relax a bit, but the first four goals didn't get the ho-hum treatment awarded to the fifth. Ticker-tape, flares, drums, noise - and that was just the neutral observers from UEFA.

Another perk of sitting where I was came in the form of free prawn sandwiches and drinks at half-time. I was sitting right by the door when they opened, and cleaned up a tray of dainty fruit pastries before many others came in. Standing with a cold beer and a plate of spicy chicken wings on the balcony outside the hospitality room, with the Ozel Tim police detachment below me, it was hard not to feel a bit of a free-loader, like the lad in the 'Live To Loaf' Strongbow ad. But somehow I handled it OK.

NUMBER 10 IS HAGI NUMBER

It was Wednesday, only three days since I'd paid the Ukrainian Interior Police to bunk off work for a bit and drive me to the airport in Kiev. For the first time, it felt a bit like 'if it's Wednesday, it must be Turkey'. As it happened, it could have been the Czech Republic instead. I'd been unsure whether I'd get into this game in Istanbul, so on a visit to Prague a fortnight earlier I'd taken the chance to get my hands on a Czech Republic-Belgium play-off ticket for the same night. But that would have meant watching Belgium for the third time, and there were some things I just couldn't bring myself to do. So I gave the ticket to a friend (who was Belgian, and presumably didn't feel the same way about his team that I did) and picked up the phone to the Turkish FA instead.

Here in Istanbul, there hadn't been time to build up contact with local fans in the way I'd done in so many other countries, so I felt I wasn't quite getting the same insights here into what made the locals get excited. This was all UEFA's fault of course, for scheduling the games so close together. In fact, with Turkey 3-0 up on the night at half-time and cruising, it was pretty damn obvious what was making the locals get excited.

Against opposition as moderate as Austria, it was hard to tell whether or not Turkey were a team of real quality, but it certainly appeared that way at times tonight. They had been in one of the easier European qualifying groups, in which Sweden had taken 26 points out of a possible 30, and Turkey 21. And when the draw for the finals was made in Marseilles a month later, Turkey would be handed the smoothest of rides through the group stage. Drawn together with Brazil, but also Costa Rica and China, it looked good for a Turkish appearance in the last 16 or even the last 8. But as we now know, they were to get even further than that, on undoubted merit. Overall there was no doubt that Turkey had come an enormous distance since those 8-0 wallopings of the 1980s. Even in the 1992-93 season, they had gone down 4-0 at Wembley, on one of Gazza's better post-knee op evenings.

So it was party time. Turkey were there, in the finals for the first time since 1954. That's a long time ago, longer even than David Seaman and Teddy Sheringham have been alive. The cars trailing flags and tooting horns as I walked back into the city were just the beginning, although in many countries that's as far as things go, and in other countries things never even get that far. No one sat in the seats in these cars, in some cases not even the drivers; they just hung out of all the windows at 40mph. In the centre, cars would suddenly stop in a 6-lane highway and all the occupants would fall out and start dancing. The people in the cars behind didn't seem to mind; in fact most of them got out and joined in. After 5 minutes or so, the police would arrive and move everyone on, but a little while later exactly the same thing would happen - another car would stop and another spontaneous party would get going in exactly the same place but with different people, only this time one of the lads on the back seat would turn out to be a practising snake-charmer, complete with an authentic-looking snake.

Even all this was comparatively understated compared to the celebrations that accompanied Turkey's steady progress through the knockout stages of the World Cup itself. Nationwide, an average 80% of the population watched Turkey's matches against Japan and then Senegal. In metropolitan areas the figure was said to be 82%, which argues an improbably high 78% football penetration among, say, goatherds in Cappadocia, but going by sheer numbers the TV figures were undoubtedly the nation's highest ever. Even while Turkey were still in the tournament, statues of Turkish squad players were being put up all over the place and streets were being renamed after them as well. Somehow you couldn't quite see a Beckham Boulevard in Manchester. Maybe in Bangkok.

Next day I took a couple of taxis around the city, so as to see some of it before my afternoon flight. There was no problem with any of the drivers' football knowledge today, there was only a problem seeing out of the cracked front windows. 'Inter Milan - they do not pay their Turkish players,' said the old bloke who drove me across the bridge over the Golden Horn inlet. We talked about Hakan Sukur's chances of finding an English club - and there were plenty chasing him, or at least interested in him, including Arsenal, Liverpool and Blackburn again - clearly Graeme Souness was putting his Turkish experience to good use. But if I needed any more proof of the degree of football knowledge that is taken for granted in Turkey, it came at the airport.

In amongst the usual globalised departure lounge duty-free tat, there were a few stalls selling local stuff. A prominently displayed row of replica football gear had, predictably enough, a selection of Galatasaray T-shirts, many with a number 10 on the back. There was no obvious price, but a little sticker on the back also said '10'. I asked the stallholder if this was the price and, optimistically, whether it meant ten dollars. Back came a look of corrosive contempt. 'No,' he said. 'Number 10 is Hagi number. That shirt costs 65 dollars.'

I went to catch my plane.

By giving me a free ticket, Turkey became the only country in Europe whose association helped me in kind, unless you counted Vlatka and Josip's unofficial help in Croatia. But everywhere I'd been, I'd encountered only friendliness, curiosity and helpfulness, and never once any aggravation or hostility for being foreign, and English to boot. Mind you, I did become a bit of a homer, wherever I happened to be: standing at the games with local fans more or less dictates that that's going to happen. Only once was it different; in Athens, when the Greek police asked no questions before lumping me in with the Germans. When in Athens, I did what the Germans did.

As I flew back across Europe, I was well aware that this was my final trip - apart from a very brief one to Germany during the World Cup Finals themselves. I'd visited quite a few parts of Europe in the year or so I spent travelling to these games, but I'd deliberately avoided the big, established football nations of western Europe. Football in regions off the beaten Champions' League track may not have the resources (either of people, or money, or both) to take on the big countries of the West but, apart from in Finland, it is as passionately supported as anywhere, at least at national level when the foreign-based stars can return. Compared with club football, international football levels the playing field significantly, giving countries like Slovenia and Denmark the chance to appear at the greatest show on earth, the World Cup Finals, allowing countries like Croatia in 1998, and Turkey in 2002, to make it to the semis; and giving a corner-taking journeyman footballer from Macedonia the opportunity to make England's David Seaman look like a complete Charlie. Sport depends on unpredictability, on not knowing what the result is going to be. Sadly, however, the money at the top of the tree in club football helps the chosen few to recruit from the world's best and to iron out uncertainty, to the detriment of the sport as a whole. Look at the 2003-04 English Premiership race for fourth place. Let's be realistic: money and its influence are here to stay, and we have to accept what it has done to the game and its players. But there is room in both life and sport for the underdog, and as long as UEFA regulations dictate that Italy or Germany still have to play the Faroe Islands in front of about 63 people in Torshavn occasionally, I'll be there, always in spirit and sometimes in person, in the hope that the underdog will have its day that day.